LONDON COUNCILS

Blue Bad~~ge~~ ~~Par~~
Guide f

CW00376665

CON~~TENTS~~

Information specific for the Blue Badge user supplied by MPIE Enterprises Ltd © 2011.
Tel: 0844 847 0875

All rights reserved www.thePIEguide.com
Special thanks for the help and support of London Councils, SOLT and TfL.

London Underground Map by permission of Transport Trading Limited Registered User No. 11/1909/P

Front Cover Image © Jason Hawkes

Disclaimer
Every possible effort has been taken to ensure that the information given in this publication is accurate, whilst the publishers would be grateful to learn of any errors, users should be aware that this information may change at any time. Parking bays, lines and signs may be moved to accommodate new traffic schemes, resurfacing, road works or many other reasons, they regret they cannot accept any responsibility for loss thereby caused.

General Enquiries & Trade Sales
Telephone: 0844 847 0875
email: info@thePIEguide.com   www.thePIEguide.com

Printed for The PIE Guide by Collins, a subsidiary of HarperCollinsPublishers Ltd.
Mapping © Collins Bartholomew 2011

ISBN 978-0-9570443-0-2
Printed in China

An easier way to go shopping without going over budget...

£10 OFF
your first online shop when you spend £50 or more by the 28th December 2014. Enter XXFFTT at the online checkout.

Tesco.com
Just like doing your weekly shop in a Tesco store. Plus...

- **Stick to your budget -** check your spend as you shop with a running total
- **Offers in one place -** all the regular in-store offers are grouped together, so it's easier to find the savings
- **Delivery to your fridge door -** 7 days a week and up to 11pm weeknights

Shop on the go from your smartphone.
Go to tesco.com/groceries

find us on

It's more rewarding with CLUBCARD

tesco.com/groceries

Dear Blue Badge Guide User

Welcome to the latest edition of London Councils Blue Badge Parking Guide. The booklet has proved popular with users, and this revised edition has built on this format and provides further information on parking in Greater London.

There is immense pressure on London's roads, not only for parking space but also for the requirements of traffic flow, and in many cases the demands in one area are very different from other places. As such, different restrictions are needed to cover these demands, so whereas holders of a Blue Badge can take advantage of certain concessions these may not always apply across the whole of London.

The aim of this Guide is to explain what concessions Blue Badge holders are able to take advantage of, and where these concessions apply.

The Guide contains a comprehensive map of Central London where the pressures are greatest, as well as maps of certain key areas in Outer London.

In addition to the maps the Guide also provides notes on using the Blue Badge throughout London, including London wide concessions, details of using your Blue Badge at airports, and information regarding the congestion charge.

The Guide also contains a directory of services that may be of benefit for Blue Badge holders.

I hope you enjoy the latest edition of the Guide. If you do have any comments please refer to the feedback section at the end of the Guide.

Yours,

Nick Lester

Corporate Director of Services
London Councils

TfL
Transport for London (TfL) manages the Tube, buses, London Overground, trams, river services, Docklands Light Railway (DLR), taxis and more. It also runs Dial-a-Ride and other travel assistance schemes. One of its main goals is to make getting around the city easier for everyone.

The Capital's 8,000 buses which run on around 700 routes across the Greater London area are fully low-floor accessible. All of London's 21,000 black cabs have wheelchair ramps. Every station and train on the DLR network is fully accessible and all new London Overground stations are step-free.

Buses
Buses are an easy way to travel around London as they are low-floor, wheelchair accessible vehicles with retractable ramps. There is room for one person using a wheelchair that is up to 70cm wide and 120cm long, weighing a maximum of 300kg. Wheelchair users are entitled to free travel and assistance dogs are welcome.

London's buses are now fitted with iBus, which features on-board "next stop" announcements. This tells you where you are, what the next stop is and where the bus is headed.

Tube
Currently 63 Tube stations are step-free and this will increase to 65 by the 2012 Games. The Tube upgrade plan is delivering improved access across the network.

The station refurbishment programme has introduced improvements such as tactile strips on platforms and staircases; platform humps, which close the gap between platform and train; wider ticket gates, so wheelchair users can travel independently; induction loops; studded surfaces; platform seating and help points.

New trains coming into service have audio and visual passenger information, plus dedicated spaces for wheelchair users. Passengers are encouraged to ask a member of staff for help if needed.

**Transport
for London**

DLR

The DLR covers parts of east and southeast London and is fully accessible. Audio and visual announcements on each train let you know the next stop and other services available, plus the final destination of the train.

The gap between the platform edge and the train is approximately 7.5cm and the step up or down from the platform to the train is around 5cm. These levels allow easier access for most passengers. Many wheelchair users find getting on and off smoothest with the largest wheel first, which may mean reversing.

Journey planning/maps and guides

Journey Planner is a free, online and easy-to-use facility to help you plan your trip. You can customise it to look for routes that, for example, avoid stairs, have a maximum walking time, are step-free or do not include a particular mode – e.g. the Tube. Visit: www.tfl.gov.uk/journeyplanner

TfL also has a wide range of maps and guides in accessible formats, including large print, audio and black and white. There are versions of the Tube map available which show stations with the fewest stairs, where toilets are located and access levels at each stop.

Visit: www.tfl.gov.uk to see the full range or call 0843 222 1234*.

A number of accessibility guides are also available on the TfL website.
These include:

> Assisted transport services
> Taxi and Private Hire guide
> Getting around London
> Making Rail Accessible: Helping Older and Disabled Passengers (large print)

If you do not have internet access, call the 24-hour travel information line on: 0843 222 1234* for a copy.

*You pay no more than 5p per minute if calling from a BT landline. There may be a connection charge. Charges from mobiles or other landline providers may vary.

fish INSURANCE

Disabled Car
Insurance

At Fish we know that every little saving helps, that's why we constantly offer competitive premiums on our Disabled Car Insurance.

Our policy is specifically designed for disabled drivers and blue badge holders, including wheelchair accessible and specially adapted vehicles.

So if you want to take advantage of Car Insurance designed for your specific needs - **now is your chance!**

Are you a Blue Badge Holder?

- ✔ Insurance for wheelchair adapted cars
- ✔ New for old cover which specifically protects modifications
- ✔ Up to £2500 wheelchair in transit cover
- ✔ Free courtesy car or up to £700 mobility allowance if a suitable car is not available
- ✔ Breakdown recovery including home start

Now includes breakdown recovery and home start as standard
Call now for a quote 0500 432141

Editor's Notes
3rd Edition – London Blue Badge Parking Guide

We are delighted by the response we received from the last edition and are proud of this new fully revised third edition of the London Blue Badge Parking Guide. We have extended the area of coverage to include the Olympic Park. After the 2012 Games, the Queen Elizabeth Olympic Park will become a unique area of London, offering visitors the best in sporting and cultural amenities, excellent transport links and parklands.

The Capital continues to evolve and the mobility of disabled people across the Capital has improved; yet there is still the constant concern of rules and regulations and how to access the facilities that are available. Journey planning in London can be a challenge especially close to your destination and our aim is to help you by providing this handy-sized comprehensive guide.

We have profiles of all London hospitals and major sporting venues for Blue Badge parking; consulted with London's main airports to fully update the contacts and travel advice, and extended the coverage of the National Key Scheme (RADAR) toilets to include 'community toilets'.

Our team has re-surveyed the Blue Badge parking information and updated all the bays and on-street parking information you need. The guide incorporates the Accessible Theatre Guide that brings together theatre facilities and parking information.

All this together with a directory of over fifty organisations that give advice and support mean this is more than just a Blue Badge parking map, but an essential guide for any Blue Badge holders in London.

Thank you to all the users of the guide, I hope it makes your life easier and becomes an essential reference for you. Please feel free feedback any comments.

Many thanks

Robert Talbot
Editor
Public Information Exchange (PIE)
robert@thepieguide.com

The Blue Badge Scheme offers special parking concessions for holders with disabilities. It allows badge holders to park close to their destination. The concessions typically apply only to on-street parking but some apply in select Car Parks (specially identified on the map). This fully updated Guide illustrates the various concessions across London and will detail the specific on-street parking options as well as detailing any other concession available close to your destination.

Blue Badge holders are entitled to parking concessions in other EU member states, and in some other European countries. The latest 'The Blue Badge Scheme: rights and responsibilities in England' leaflet, available from the Department for Transport, explains the concessions and lists all the countries.

Local Badge schemes in Central London

You may be aware that within Central London the following boroughs have their own registered disabled badge scheme for residents as well as their business residents; Westminster (white badge), City of London (red badge), Kensington and Chelsea (purple badge) and part of Camden (green badge). These bays have not been marked on the map as they are typically assigned. The background mapping colour will help you determine which on-street options you are permitted to park on within these and all other boroughs that have some differences to the normal rules.

On-street parking concessions

Listed below are the various on-street parking options for Blue Badge holders. As mentioned above some of the concessions vary across the London Boroughs. This Guide illustrates, based on your destination point, what the on-street parking concessions are. Either use the maps background colour coding to assess if parking is permitted or refer to the table on pages 100-101. The on-street parking options include;

Single & double yellow lines

A Blue Badge holder is permitted to park on single or double yellow lines in most areas, up to 3 hours typically, except where loading restrictions apply. Note some London Authorities restrict this concession. These areas are colour coded within the map. You must ensure you are not causing an obstruction. Use your clock to indicate your arrival time.

Pay & Display or metered parking

Payment for parking on Pay & Display or meters (where they still exist) does apply in some areas within London. Certain Borough's provide a period of time free of charge once an initial payment has been made. Please note Pay & Display machines often do not give any information on the concessions for Blue Badge holders. The Pay & Display machines do indicate which Borough they belong to. Please note if your disability prevents you reaching the slot to put your money in, you will need to write to the council to explain this if you get a ticket.

Cashless/Mobile phone payment for Pay & Display (Pay by Phone)

Some councils have introduced cashless payment for Pay & Display parking. For councils where payment is required by Blue Badge holders you still get the free period of time but the payment needs to be made via mobile phone. You will need to register in advance and set up an account. There are some bays that are only payable by mobile so be careful if you do not have a mobile or have not pre-registered. Note that until we get a centralised scheme you are likely to need to register with each council that operates a Pay by Phone scheme. You will still need to display your Blue Badge.

Blue Badge parking bays

You may park without time restriction for free in Blue Badge parking bays that have no maximum stay. Some Blue Badge bays will show a time limit

that you must observe. Please note on our map we put the number of hours maximum stay within the symbol. Where it is marked 'U' this means unlimited (no maximum time limit) and where they are marked with a '!' this means check signs locally as times vary.

Red Route box bays

Red Routes prohibit parking for Blue Badge holders within the controlling hours. The red boxes marked on the road indicate that parking, or loading is permitted during the off peak times, normally between 10am and 4pm.
There are specific red route parking box bays which have no time limits and red route loading box bays that typically provide a maximum of 3 hours stay for Blue Badge holders. Ensure you check this time limit and try not to use these during the rush hours.

Residents' parking

Residents' parking provides the largest area of parking spaces within London and is readily distributed across most areas. Not all residents' spaces are free to use for Blue Badge holders. Use the maps background colour coding to assess if parking in Residents parking bays is permitted at your destination point. If in any doubt do not park in a Residents bay.

Shared use bay

Shared use bays in some Boroughs are a combination of Pay & Display as well as Residents parking. Use the map

P
Mon-Sat
8.30am-6.30pm
Permit holders **XXX**
or
Pay at machine
→
Display ticket

background colour to assess if parking in Shared use bays is permitted at your destination point.

Where NOT to park

Red Routes

Red Routes mark out London's important roads identified by the red no-stopping lines or signs along the route. You can only stop briefly to set down or pick up the badge holder. Stopping to set down other non-disabled passengers is not permitted. Taxis are also permitted to drop down and pick up on Red Routes. There are Red Route parking bays available on these routes for parking, please check the signs for the concession times.

Loading bans

Loading bans are shown by a single or double stripe on the kerb. Please ensure you do not park here. You are permitted to pick up or set down a passenger. Loading bans in London are typically on junctions, corners and the entrance or exit of streets. The double stripes indicate no loading at any time while the single stripe should have a post mounted plate indicating

No loading at any time	No loading Mon-Sat 8.30am-6.30pm

the times no loading/unloading is permitted. If there is an arrow on the sign, it indicates the direction prohibition starts. Best to avoid.

Pedestrian areas

Please note in pedestrian areas, waiting and loading restrictions may be in force even where there are no yellow lines shown on the road or stripes on the kerb. The restrictions in force should be shown on plates displayed at the kerbside. This map has highlighted most of the pedestrian streets as well as the streets used for markets.

Clearways

Some areas are protected by clearway restrictions at certain times (check the plate). On a clearway stopping is not permitted and there is no concession for Blue Badge holders.

Double white lines in the centre of the road

Should there be solid double white lines or even broken white lines you are typically not permitted to park on that street.

Others areas NOT permitted to park include;

- Bus lanes and bus stops during the hours of operation. You are allowed to enter a bus lane to pick up and set down. There may be some kerbside restrictions so keep an eye on these. The distance driven in the bus lane needs to be minimal and you cannot enter any bus lane that is 'Bus-only routes'. CCTV is used to enforce these lanes so ensure your Blue Badge is visible.

- Cycle lanes or pavements, footways or verges (except in areas where there are signs showing it is legal).

- On any pedestrian crossing that includes Zebra, Pelican, Toucan (for bicycles) and Puffin crossings.

- Next to any dropped footway either across a driveway or where the kerb has been lowered for pedestrians to cross.

- On zig-zag markings used typically before and after pedestrian crossings or school entrances and on markings where is it is written **KEEP CLEAR**.

- Blue Badge rules do **NOT** often apply at airports - see airport section for parking options.

Other Bay types NOT permitted to park

Do not park in suspended bays (shown by a yellow no parking sign or cones) or business, trader, doctor, police, diplomat, ambulance, motorcycle, or similar bays including taxi ranks. Blue Badge holders are not permitted to use dedicated disabled badge holder bays

(indicated by a sign or painted on the street), often with a permit number painted by it.

Hazardous places to even think about parking:

You must also ensure you do **NOT** park where it would endanger, obstruct or inconvenience pedestrians or other road users.
This includes.

- On a bend in a road

- Near the brow of a hill or hump back bridge

- School entrances and bus stops

- Close to junctions where it would make it difficult for others to see clearly

- By a traffic island, road works etc. where you would make the road much narrower

- Blocking vehicle entrances, particularly emergency vehicles

- Where the kerb has been lowered or road raised to help wheelchair users

Important to know

Your vehicle cannot legally be wheel clamped on the public highway for parking offences provided a valid Blue Badge  is correctly displayed. Be aware that if you park improperly on privately owned land you may risk having your vehicle clamped. If you park where it would cause an obstruction or be a danger to other road users your vehicle could be removed. You could also be prosecuted and your badge withdrawn. CCTV is being used extensively for bus lanes and parking contraventions enforcement. The cameras may not always pick out the Blue Badge and it is more than likely you will need to appeal these tickets. The cameras also capture moving traffic offences which Blue Badge holders are not exempt from.

What to do if?

- Blue Badge is stolen – report the theft immediately to the Police. The crime reference is likely to be required before a replacement badge can be issued.

- Towed away or clamped – If your Blue Badge is displayed you should not be clamped or towed away even if you park illegally. If the vehicle is causing an obstruction it may be repositioned, but usually to a nearby street.

- Car is missing – If your vehicle is missing call the **TRACE** service **020 7747 4747** (24 hours). They will be able to confirm if it has been towed away and where it has been removed to.

- You get a Parking Ticket, Red Route or Bus lane violation (Penalty Charge Notices or PCN) – do not ignore it. You may have to pay more if you do not either pay or contest the ticket promptly. If you want to contest the ticket write to the council concerned.

PENALTY CHARGE NOTICE

Fixed Penalty Notices (FPN) are issued by the Police. If you want to contest the ticket you must ask for a court hearing by typically writing to the address on the back of the ticket. Visit: **www.tfl.gov.uk/roadusers** for more information on road regulation within London.

Your Blue Badge

It is your responsibility to ensure that the badge is used properly. It is in your own interest that the badge should retain the respect of other motorists. Please play your part.

Do not allow others to use your Blue Badge – this is a criminal offence. To reduce the risk of this happening accidentally, you should remove the badge whenever you are not using the parking concessions.

You must ensure that the details on the front of the badge remain legible. If they become unreadable, the badge must be returned to the local authority to be re-issued.

Ensure you set your clock and display your badge and clock clearly on the dashboard or facia panel where it can be read through the front windscreen.

New Blue Badge design

From January 2012 the new badge design is issued to all new badge applicants, those renewing and those replacing badges that may have been lost or stolen. The old style badge will still be valid to use by badge holders until the date they expire, which could be December 2014.

The new badge design includes raised text features, a hologram and withstands up to 120 degrees centigrade. An up-to-date photograph of the badge holder must be submitted and is digitally scanned on the back of an individual badge.

Abuse of the Blue Badge Scheme

There are several ways in which Blue Badges can be misused. These include:

- Use of the badge when no longer valid.
- Misuse of a valid badge by a friend or relative, with or without the badge holder's knowledge or permission.
- Use by the holder of a badge that has been reported lost or stolen – possibly to obtain another badge for a friend or relative.
- Use of a stolen or copied badge by the thief, forger or someone who has acquired it from them.

The most significant change to the regulations, from an enforcement perspective, is in respect of the ability to withdraw a badge for misuse.

Power to inspect

Police officers, traffic wardens, parking attendants and civil enforcement officers have the power to inspect any Blue Badge being used.

These people should produce an identity card with a photograph to prove who they are. If they ask to see your badge, you must show it to them, if not, you are breaking the law and could be fined up to £1000. Only a Police Officer has the power to seize and confiscate lost, stolen, fraudulent, invalid and misused badges.

The serial number printed on the badge identifies the month and year of birth and a code indicates the gender of the holder.

Security against Blue Badge theft

Every year thousands of disability parking permits are being stolen that cost Blue Badge holders a replacement broken window and the hassle claiming and waiting for a replacement badge. Ensure your badge is not an easy target to be stolen. When the badge is not required ensure it is kept safely away and out of sight. When you need to use the Badge ensure it is secured within a protective device.

The Blue Badge Protector secures the badge to the car within a metal frame with a lock that feeds through the steering wheel that provides a simple and effective deterrent when parked on the street.

To order the Blue Badge Protector call **0844 847 0875** or order online **www.bluebadgeprotector.com**. Some local authorities often give these protectors to resident Blue Badge holders.

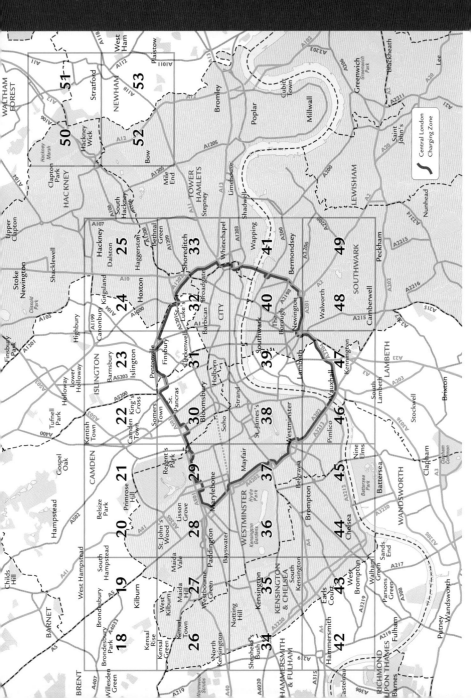

Blue Badge Parking Concessions by London Borough

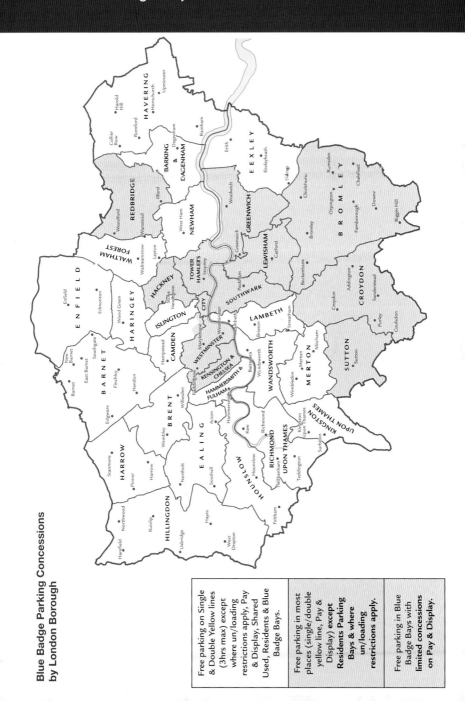

Free parking on Single & Double Yellow lines (3hrs max) except where un/loading restrictions apply, Pay & Display, Shared Used, Residents & Blue Badge Bays.

Free parking in most places (single/double yellow line, Pay & Display) except **Residents Parking Bays & where un/loading restrictions apply.**

Free parking in Blue Badge Bays with limited concessions on Pay & Display.

16 Key to map symbols

Symbol	Description	Symbol	Description
Dual **A1**	Primary route		Administration & law
Dual **A40**	'A' road		Hospital
B519	'B' road		Industry & commerce
	Other road/Toll		Leisure & tourism
A1	Red route		Major office
	Street market		Cemetery
	Restricted access road		Public open space
	Pedestrian street		Wood/Forest
	Cycle path		Main railway station
	Track/Footpath		Other national railway station
→	One way street		London Overground station
	Congestion zone		London Underground station
	Bus/Coach station		Docklands Light Railway station
			Tramlink station
			Pedestrian ferry landing stage

Colours refer to the background colour of the mapping. Also see page 15.

Free parking on Single & Double Yellow lines (3hrs max) except where un/loading restrictions apply, Pay & Display, Shared Used, Residents & Blue Badge Bays.

Free parking in most places (single/double yellow line, Pay & Display) **except Residents Parking Bays & where un/loading restrictions apply.**

Free parking in Blue Badge Bays with **limited concessions on Pay & Display.**

SCALE 1:13,000   4.9 inches to 1 mile/7.7 cm to 1 km

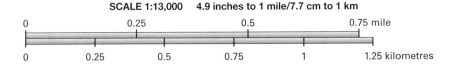

Blue Badge related symbols

Shopmobility   Theatre

Petrol stations

Petrol station

Petrol station with accessible toilet for the disabled

Petrol station with service call

Petrol station with service call with accessible toilet for the disabled

Toilets

Public toilet

National Key Scheme toilet

Wheelchair accessible public toilet

On Street Parking

Blue Badge parking bay

Red Route box bay

Character within circle refers to parking duration e.g

3 hours   4 hours

unlimited   check signs locally

Off Street Parking

P   Car park (no discount to Blue Badge holders)

D   Car park free or discounted for Blue Badge holders

P   Car park with height restriction of **2.20m** or less (no discount to Blue Badge holders)

D   Car park with height restrictions free or discounted for Blue Badge holders

Definition of accessibility grading used by car parks

D1   Accessible to a wheelchair-user travelling independently.

D2   Accessible to a wheelchair-user travelling with assistance.

D3   Accessible to a wheelchair-user or someone with limited mobility, able to walk a few paces and up a max of three steps.

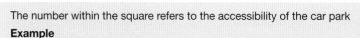

The number within the square refers to the accessibility of the car park

Example

D1   represents a car park discounted for Blue Badge holders and is accessible to a wheelchair-user travelling independently.

 represents a car park with a height restriction of **2.20m** or less. The car park is discounted for Blue Badge holders and is accessible to a wheelchair-user travelling with assistance.

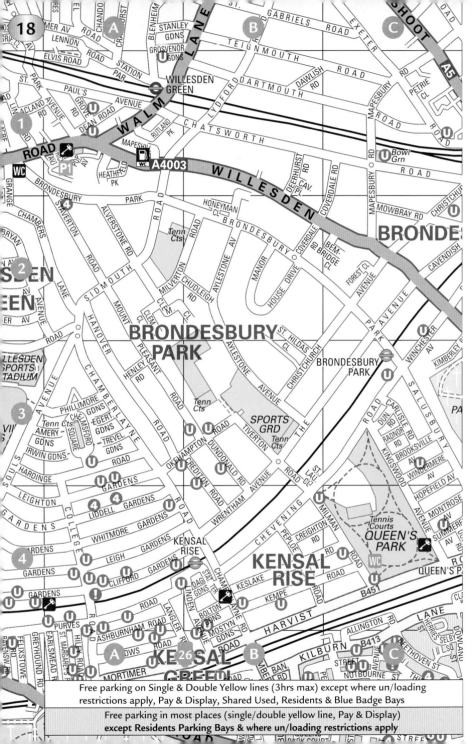

Free parking on Single & Double Yellow lines (3hrs max) except where un/loading restrictions apply, Pay & Display, Shared Used, Residents & Blue Badge Bays

Free parking in most places (single/double yellow line, Pay & Display) except Residents Parking Bays & where un/loading restrictions apply

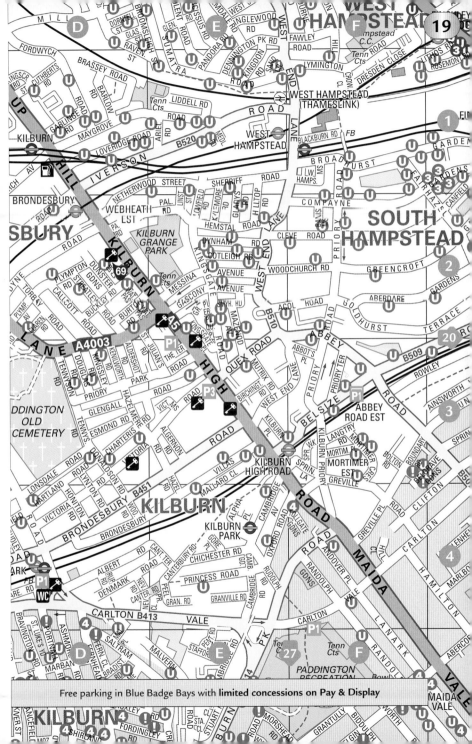

WEST HAMPSTEAD

SOUTH HAMPSTEAD

KILBURN

BRONDESBURY

SBURY

WEST HAMPSTEAD
(THAMESLINK)

WEST HAMPSTEAD

KILBURN GRANGE PARK

KILBURN HIGH ROAD

KILBURN PARK

PADDINGTON OLD CEMETERY

PADDINGTON RECREATION

MAIDA VALE

Free parking in Blue Badge Bays with **limited concessions on Pay & Display**

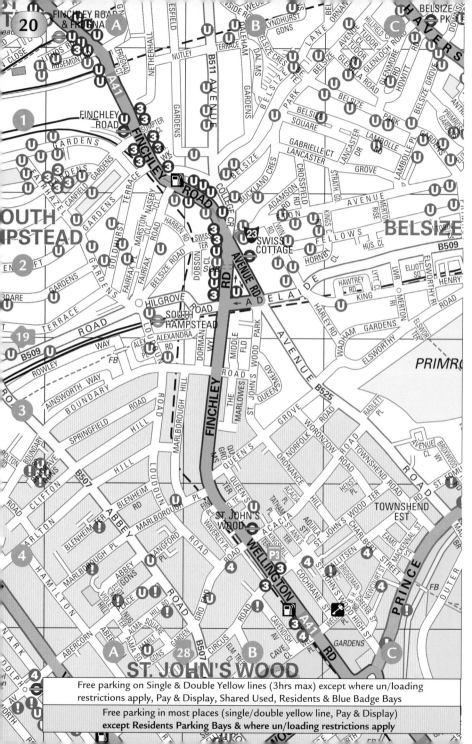

Free parking on Single & Double Yellow lines (3hrs max) except where un/loading
restrictions apply, Pay & Display, Shared Used, Residents & Blue Badge Bays

Free parking in most places (single/double yellow line, Pay & Display)
except Residents Parking Bays & where un/loading restrictions apply

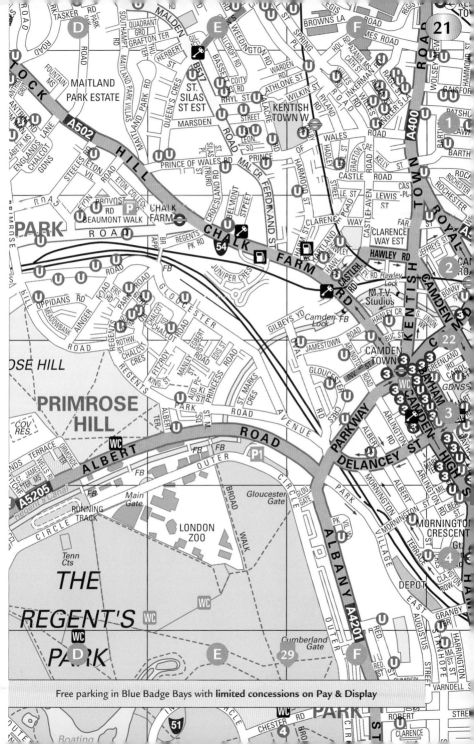

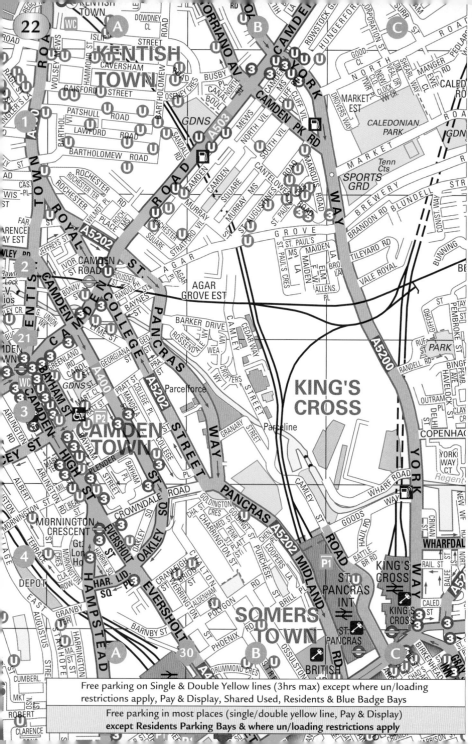

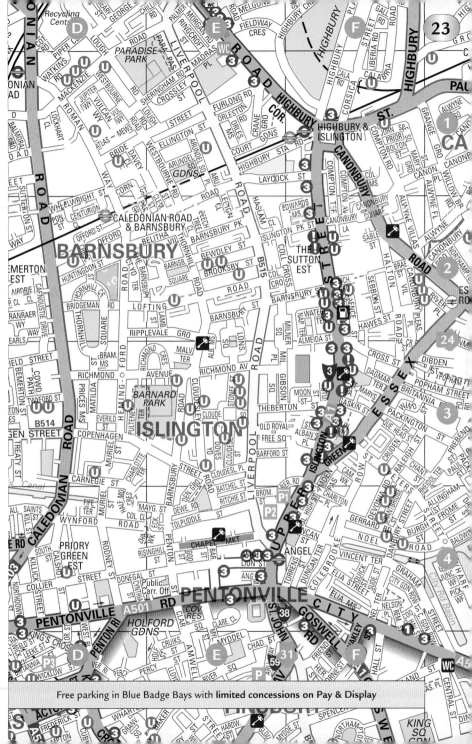

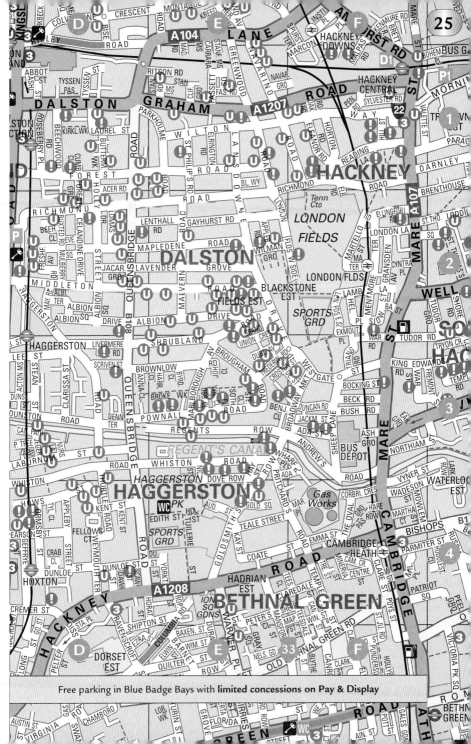

Free parking in Blue Badge Bays with **limited concessions on Pay & Display**

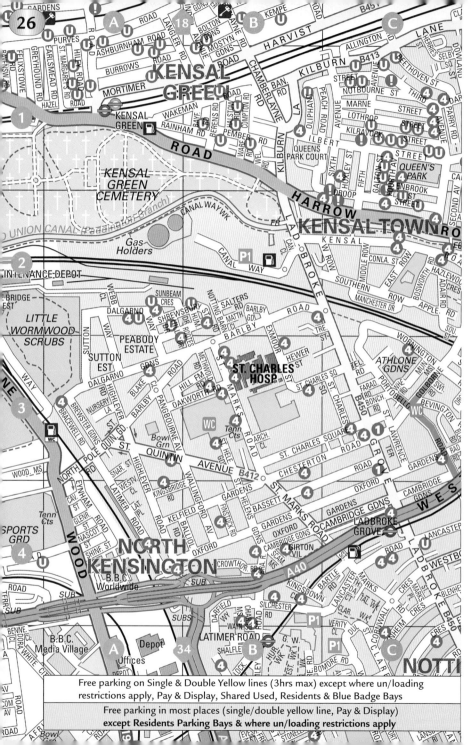

26

Free parking on Single & Double Yellow lines (3hrs max) except where un/loading restrictions apply, Pay & Display, Shared Used, Residents & Blue Badge Bays

Free parking in most places (single/double yellow line, Pay & Display) except Residents Parking Bays & where un/loading restrictions apply

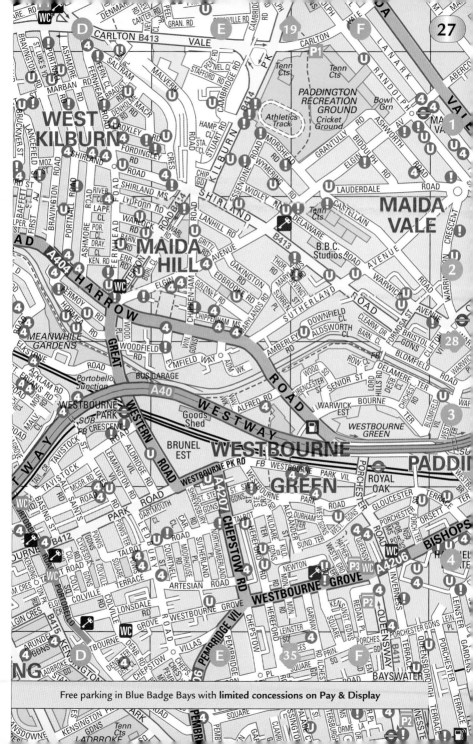

WEST KILBURN

MAIDA HILL

MAIDA VALE

PADDINGTON RECREATION GROUND

Cricket Ground.

Athletics Track

Tenn Cts

Bowl Grn

B.B.C. Studios

MEANWHILE GARDENS

Portobello Junction

BUS GARAGE

Goods Shed

BRUNEL EST

WESTBOURNE PARK

WESTWAY

WESTBOURNE GREEN

PADDIN

ROYAL OAK

WESTBOURNE GREEN

BISHOPS

WESTBOURNE GROVE

BAYSWATER

Free parking in Blue Badge Bays with **limited concessions on Pay & Display**

Free parking on Single & Double Yellow lines (3hrs max) except where un/loading restrictions apply, Pay & Display, Shared Used, Residents & Blue Badge Bays

Free parking in most places (single/double yellow line, Pay & Display) except Residents Parking Bays & where un/loading restrictions apply

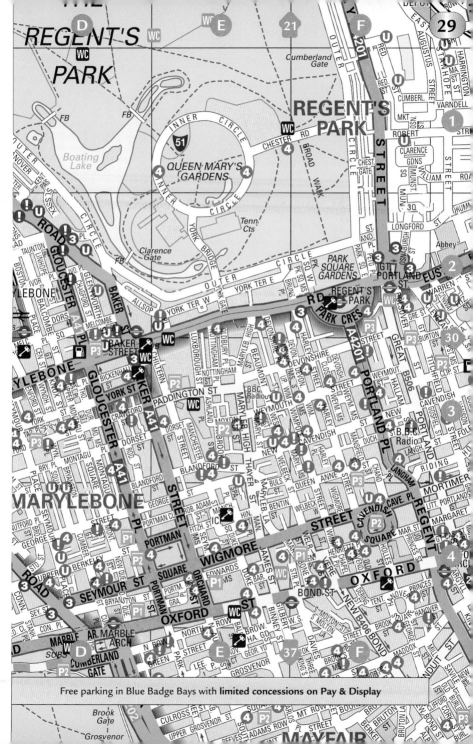

THE
REGENT'S
PARK

REGENT'S
PARK

QUEEN MARY'S
GARDENS

Boating
Lake

Cumberland
Gate

MARYLEBONE

MARBLE
ARCH

OXFORD
ST

OXFORD

BOND-ST

MAYFAIR

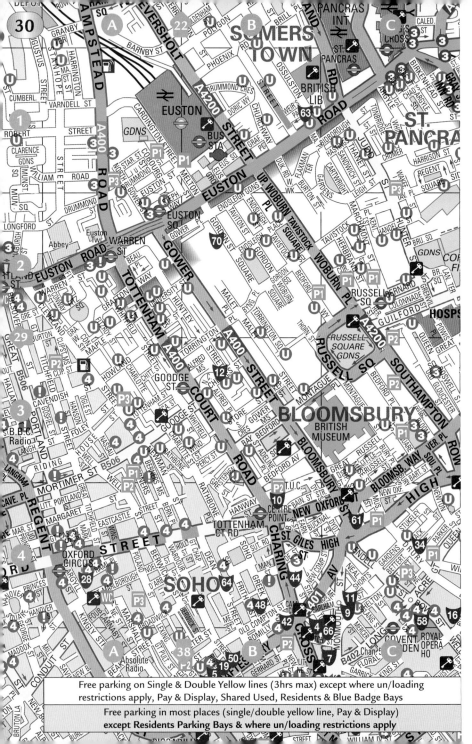

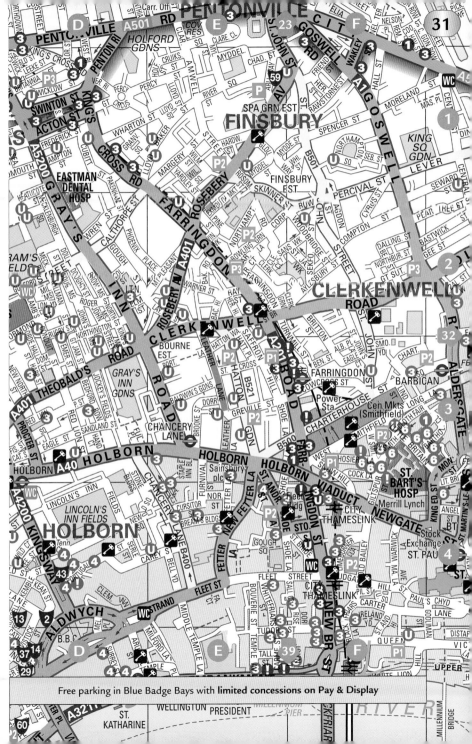

Free parking in Blue Badge Bays with **limited concessions on Pay & Display**

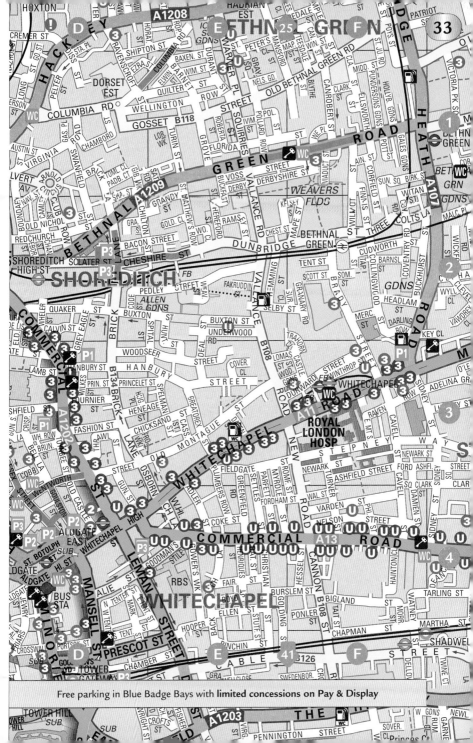

Free parking in Blue Badge Bays with limited concessions on Pay & Display

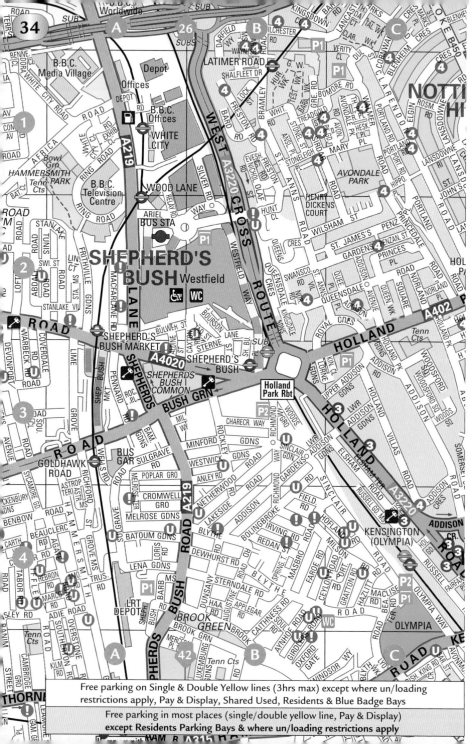

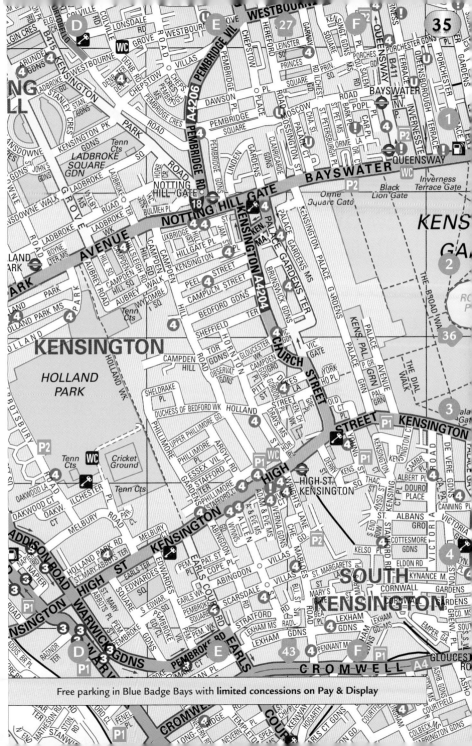

Free parking in Blue Badge Bays with **limited concessions on Pay & Display**

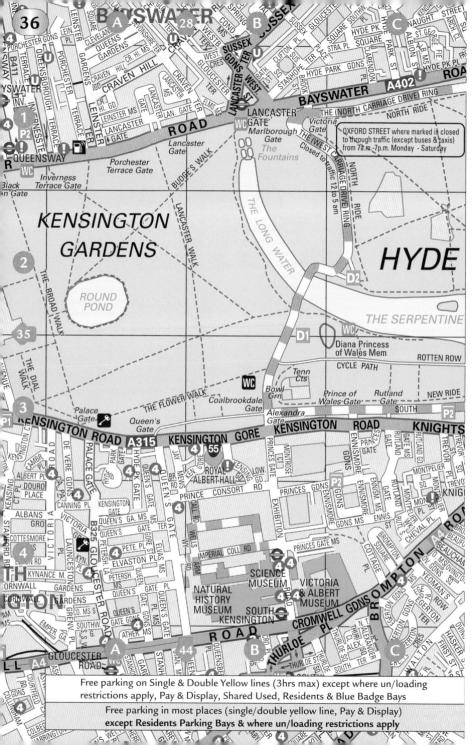

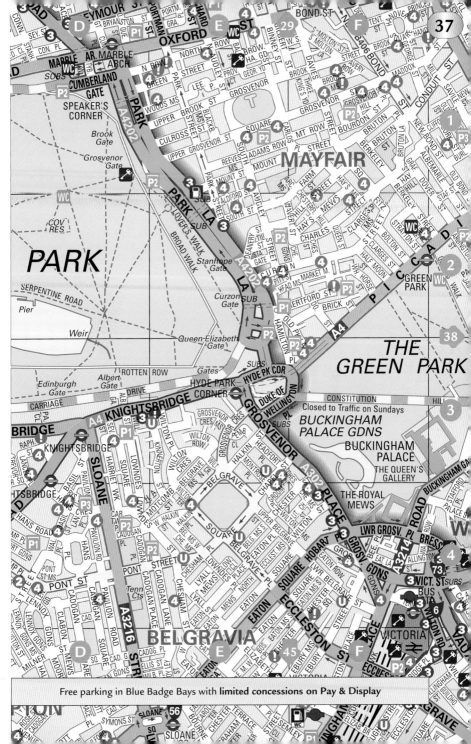

Free parking in Blue Badge Bays with **limited concessions on Pay & Display**

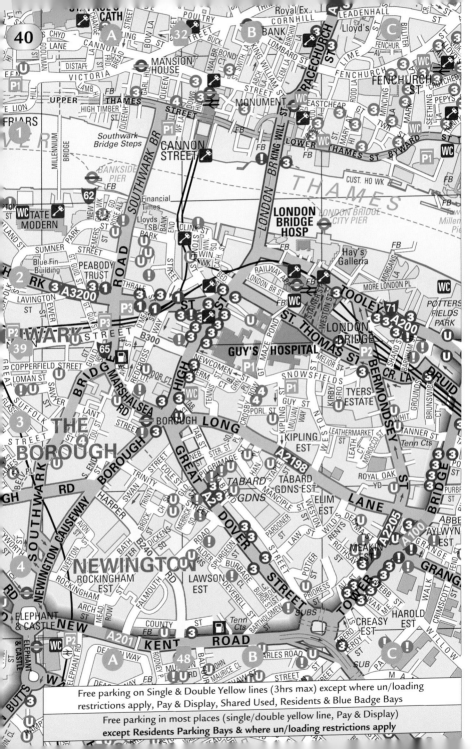

Free parking on Single & Double Yellow lines (3hrs max) except where un/loading
restrictions apply, Pay & Display, Shared Used, Residents & Blue Badge Bays
Free parking in most places (single/double yellow line, Pay & Display)
except Residents Parking Bays & where un/loading restrictions apply

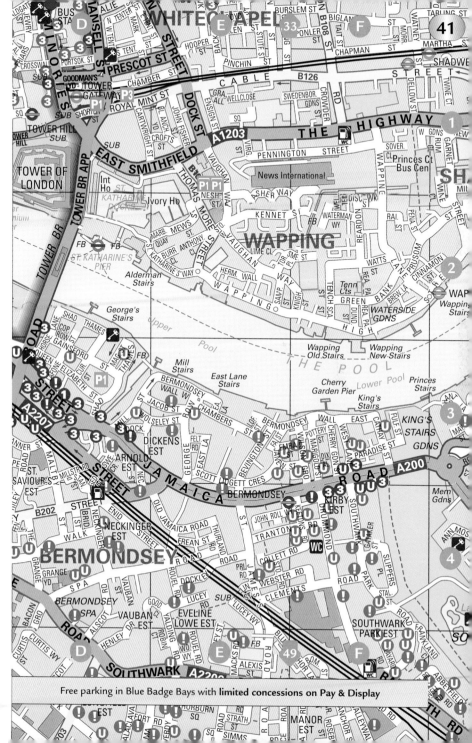

WHITECHAPEL

WAPPING

BERMONDSEY

TOWER OF LONDON

THE HIGHWAY

THE POOL

Upper Pool

Lower Pool

KING'S STAIRS GDNS

SOUTHWARK PARK EST

News International

Free parking in Blue Badge Bays with **limited concessions on Pay & Display**

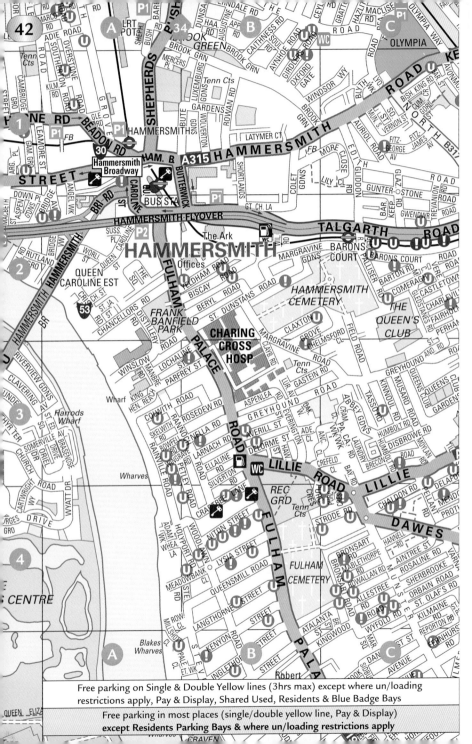

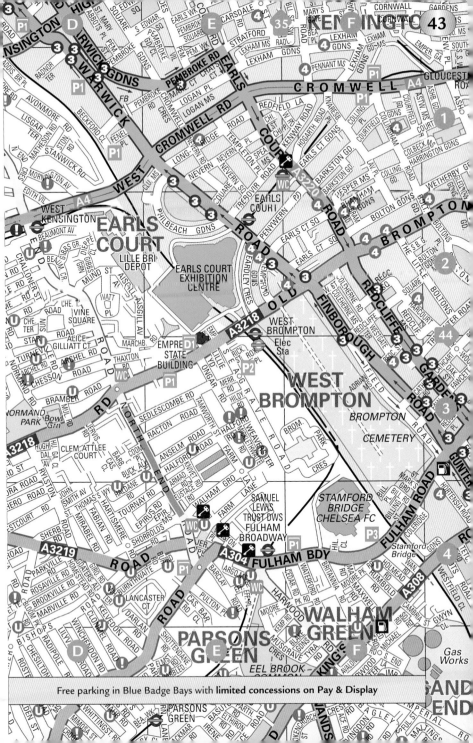

Free parking in Blue Badge Bays with **limited concessions on Pay & Display**

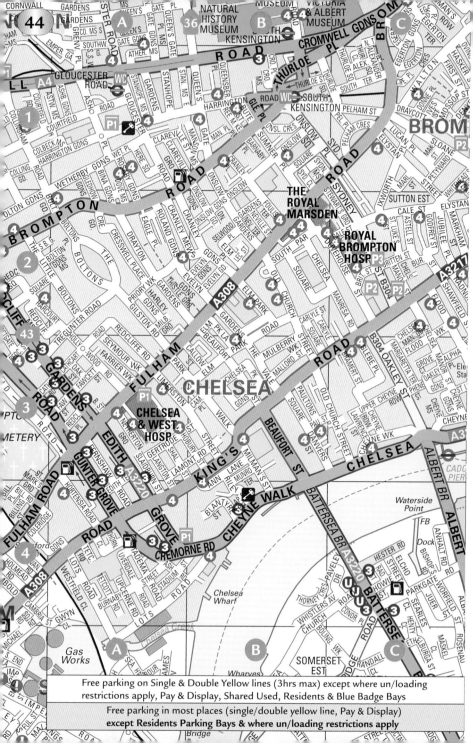

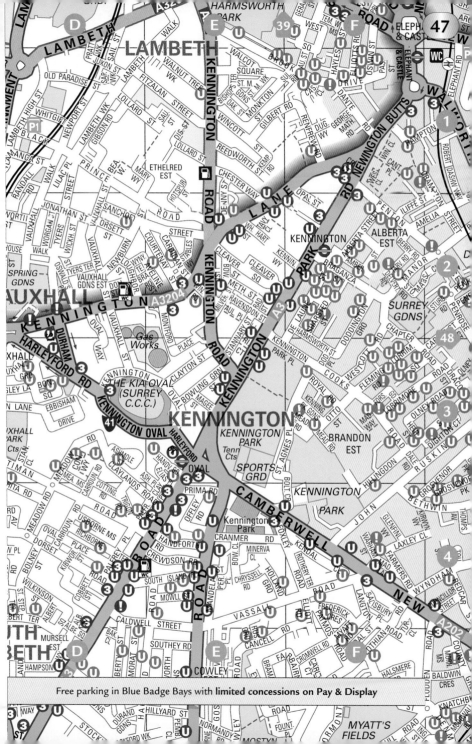

Free parking in Blue Badge Bays with **limited concessions on Pay & Display**

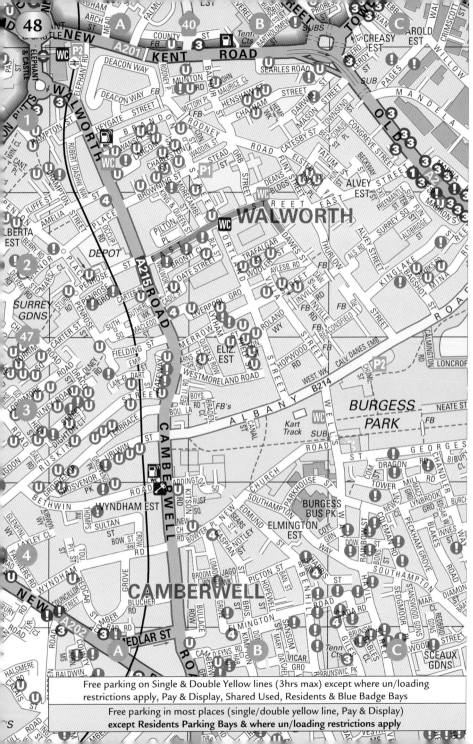

Free parking on Single & Double Yellow lines (3hrs max) except where un/loading restrictions apply, Pay & Display, Shared Used, Residents & Blue Badge Bays

Free parking in most places (single/double yellow line, Pay & Display) except Residents Parking Bays & where un/loading restrictions apply

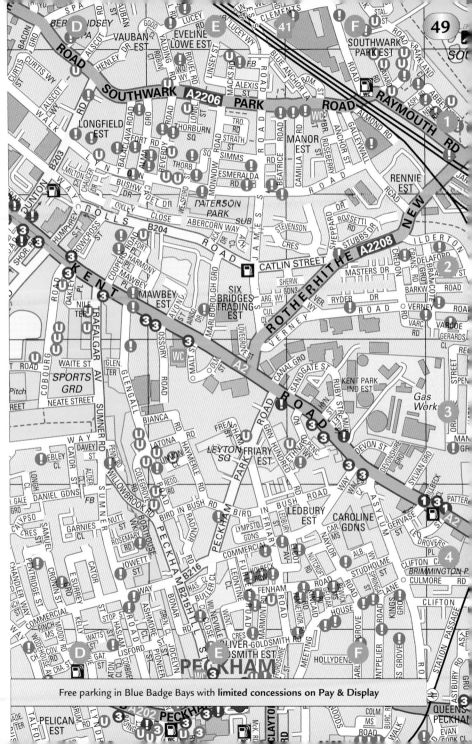

41

SPA
BER IDSEY
D
BACON
CURTIS WY
CURTIS WY
ROAD
VAUBAN EST
DR
LUCEY
LUCEY WY
RD
EVELINE
LOWE EST
E
CLEMENTS ST
SOUTHWARK
PARK EST
F

SOUTHWARK
A2206
PARK
ROAD
RAYMOUTH RD

NEW
ROTHERHITHE A2208
ILDERTON

LONGFIELD
EST

MANOR
EST

RENNIE
EST

2

PATERSON
PARK

B204
CATLIN STREET

SIX
BRIDGES
TRADING
EST

MASTERS DR

KENT
ROAD

MAWBEY
EST

KENT PARK
IND EST

Gas
Work

3

SPORTS
GRD

NEATE STREET

BIANCA

LEYTON
SQ

FRIARY
EST

LEDBURY
EST

CAROLINE
GDNS

BRIMMINGTON P

4

PENTRIDGE WAY
COMMERCIAL

D
PECKHAM
GOLDSMITH EST
E
HOLLYDENE
F

Free parking in Blue Badge Bays with **limited concessions on Pay & Display**

PELICAN
EST
PECKHAM
A202
PECKHAM
QUEENS
PECKHAM

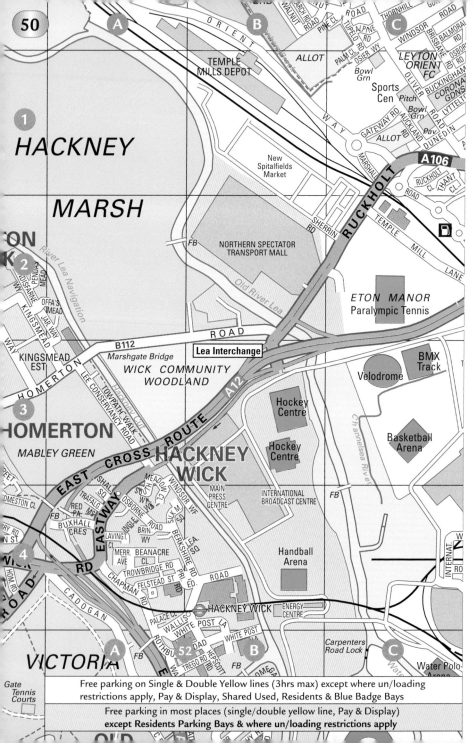

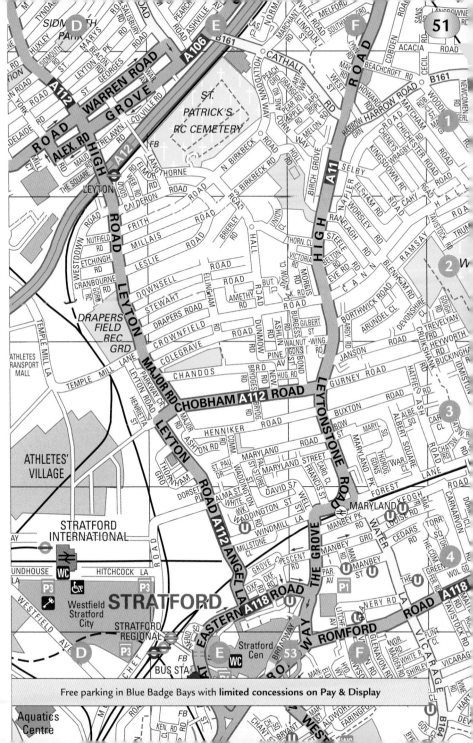

Free parking in Blue Badge Bays with **limited concessions on Pay & Display**

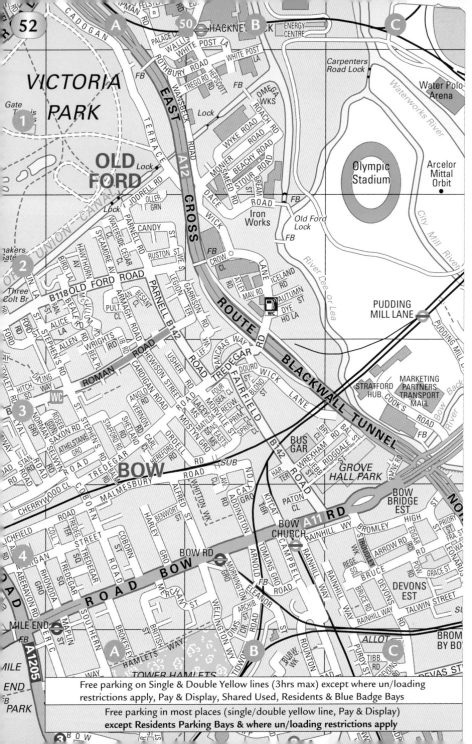

52

50 **HACKNEY**

VICTORIA PARK

OLD FORD

BOW

OLD FORD ROAD

PARNELL ROAD B142

ROMAN ROAD

TREDEGAR ROAD

BLACKWALL TUNNEL

FAIRFIELD ROAD

MALMESBURY ROAD

BOW ROAD

BOW ROAD

A11 RD

A1205

MILE END

GROVE HALL PARK

Olympic Stadium

Water Polo Arena

Arcelor Mittal Orbit

PUDDING MILL LANE

MARKETING PARTNERS TRANSPORT MALL

STRATFORD HUB

BOW BRIDGE EST

DEVONS EST

BOW CHURCH

Iron Works

Old Ford Lock

Carpenters Road Lock

ENERGY CENTRE

TOWER HAMLETS

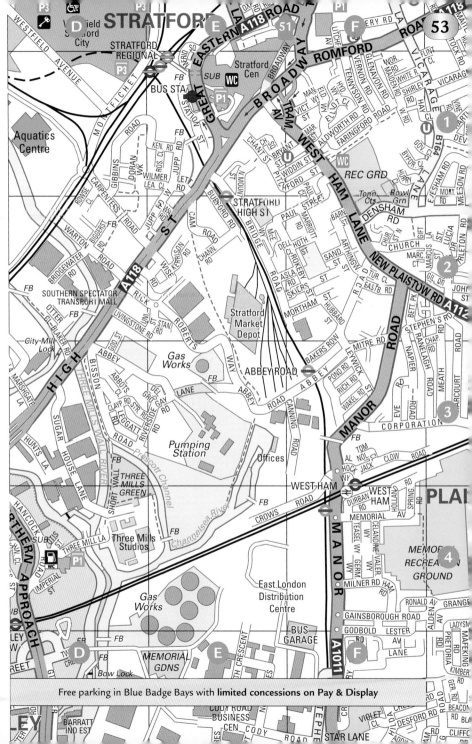

INDEX TO STREET NAMES

General Abbreviations

All	Alley	Dws	Dwellings	Hts	Heights	Ri	Rise
App	Approach	E	East	Ind	Industrial	S	South
Arc	Arcade	Embk	Embankment	Junct	Junction	Sch	School
Av	Avenue	Est	Estate	La	Lane	Shop	Shopping
Bdy	Broadway	Ex	Exchange	Lo	Lodge	Sq	Square
Bldgs	Buildings	Fld	Field	Mans	Mansions	St.	Saint
Br	Bridge	Flds	Fields	Mkt	Market	St	Street
Cen	Central, Centre	Fm	Farm	Mkts	Markets	Sta	Station
Ch	Church	Gdn	Garden	Ms	Mews	Ter	Terrace
Chyd	Churchyard	Gdns	Gardens	Mt	Mount	Trd	Trading
Circ	Circus	Gra	Grange	N	North	Twr	Tower
Cl	Close	Grd	Ground	Par	Parade	Vil	Villas
Cor	Corner	Grds	Grounds	Pas	Passage	Vw	View
Cotts	Cottages	Grn	Green	Pk	Park	W	West
Cres	Crescent	Gro	Grove	Pl	Place	Wd	Wood
Ct	Court	Gt	Great	Prec	Precinct	Wf	Wharf
Ctyd	Courtyard	Ho	House	Pt	Point	Wk	Walk
Dr	Drive	Hos	Houses	Rd	Road	Yd	Yard

Notes

The figures and letters following a street name indicate the Postal District, page and map square where the name can be found.

A

Abbey Gdns NW8	20	A4	Addington Sq SE5	48	A4	Albert Rd NW6	19	D4
Abbey Gdns W6	42	C3	Addison Av W11	34	C2	Albert Sq E15	51	F3
Abbey La E15	53	D3	Addison Br Pl W14	43	D1	Albert Sq SW8	47	D4
Abbey Orchard St SW1	38	B4	Addison Cres W14	34	C4	Albert St NW1	21	F3
Abbey Rd E15	53	F3	Addison Gdns W14	34	B4	Albert Ter NW1	21	E3
Abbey Rd NW6	19	F2	Addison Pl W11	34	C2	Albert Way SE15	49	F4
Abbey Rd NW8	20	A4	Addison Rd W14	35	D4	Alberta Est SE17	47	F2
Abbey Rd Est NW8	19	F3	Adelaide Rd E10	50	C1	Alberta St SE17	47	F2
Abbey St SE1	40	C4	Adelaide Rd NW3	20	B2	Albion Dr E8	25	D2
Abbot St E8	25	D1	Adeline Pl WC1	30	B3	Albion Ms N1	23	E3
Abbot's Pl NW6	19	F3	Adeney Cl W6	42	B3	Albion Ms W2	28	C4
Abbots Manor Est SW1	45	F1	Adie Rd W6	34	A4	Albion Pl EC1	31	F3
Abbotsbury Cl E15	53	D3	Adler St E1	33	E4	Albion Riverside Bldg SW11	44	C4
Abbotsbury Rd W14	34	C3	Admiral Wk W9	27	E3	Albion Sq E8	25	D2
Abchurch La EC4	40	B1	Adpar St W2	28	B2	Albion St W2	28	C4
Abercorn Cl NW8	28	A1	Adrian Ms SW10	43	F3	Albion Ter E8	25	D2
Abercorn Pl NW8	28	A1	Agar Gro NW1	22	A2	Aldbridge St SE17	48	C2
Abercorn Way SE1	49	E2	Agar Gro Est NW1	22	B2	Aldebert Ter SW8	46	C4
Aberdare Gdns NW6	19	F2	Agar Pl NW1	22	A2	Aldenham St NW1	22	B4
Aberdeen Pl NW8	28	B2	Agar St WC2	38	C1	Alder Cl SE15	49	D3
Aberdour St SE1	48	C1	Agate Rd W6	34	A4	Aldermanbury EC2	32	A4
Abingdon Rd W8	35	E4	Agdon St EC1	31	F2	Alderney Ms SE1	40	B4
Abingdon St SW1	38	C4	Agricola Ct E3	52	A2	Alderney St SW1	45	F1
Abingdon Vil W8	35	E4	Ainger Rd NW3	21	D2	Aldersgate St EC1	32	A3
Acacia Ms E8	20	B4	Ainsdale Dr SE1	49	E2	Aldershot Rd NW6	19	D3
Acacia Rd NW8	20	B4	Ainsley St E2	33	F1	Alford St W1	37	E2
Academy Gdns W8	35	E3	Ainsworth Way NW8	20	A3	Aldgate EC3	32	C4
Acanthus Dr SE1	49	E2	Aintree St SW6	42	C4	Aldgate High St EC3	33	D4
Achilles Cl SE1	49	E2	Air St W1	38	A1	Aldine St W12	34	A3
Acklam Rd W10	27	D3	Airdrie Cl N1	23	D2	Aldridge Rd Vil W11	27	D3
Acol Rd NW6	19	E2	Aisgill Av W14	43	D2	Aldsworth Cl W9	27	F2
Acton Ms E8	25	D3	Alan Hocken Way E15	53	F3	Aldworth Rd E15	53	F1
Acton St WC1	31	D1	Albany Mans SW11	44	C4	Aldwych WC2	39	D1
Ada Pl E2	25	E3	Albany Rd SE17	48	B3	Alexander Pl SW7	44	C1
Ada St SE5	48	C4	Albany Rd SE5	48	B3	Alexander Sq SW3	44	C1
Ada St E8	25	F3	Albany St NW1	21	F4	Alexander St W2	27	E4
Adair Rd W10	26	C2	Albemarle St W1	37	F1	Alexandra Pl NW8	20	A3
Adam & Eve Ms W8	35	E4	Albert Av SW8	47	D4	Alexandra Rd E10	51	D1
Adam St WC2	38	C1	Albert Br Rd SW11	44	C4	Alexandra Rd NW8	20	A2
Adam Wk SW6	42	A4	Albert Br SW11	44	C3	Alexis St SE16	49	E1
Adams Row W1	37	E1	Albert Br SW3	44	C3	Alfred Ms W1	30	B3
Adamson Rd NW3	20	B2	Albert Embk SE1	46	C2	Alfred Pl WC1	30	B3
Addington Rd E3	52	B4	Albert Gate SW1	37	D3	Alfred Rd W2	27	E3
			Albert Pl W8	35	F3	Alfred St E3	52	A4

Name	Page	Grid
Rossmore Rd NW1	28	C2
Rothbury Rd E9	52	A1
Rotherfield St N1	24	A2
Rotherhithe New Rd SE16	49	E2
Rothery Ter SW9	47	F4
Rothsay St SE1	40	C4
Rothwell St NW1	21	D3
Rotten Row SW1	37	D3
Rotten Row SW7	36	C3
Rouel Rd SE16	41	E4
Roundhouse Ln	50	C4
Roupell St SE1	39	E2
Rousden St NW1	22	A2
Rowallan Rd SW6	42	C4
Rowan Rd W6	42	B1
Rowberry Cl SW6	42	A4
Rowcross St SE1	49	D2
Rowington Cl W2	27	F3
Rowley Way NW8	19	F3
Rowse Cl E15	53	D2
Roxby Pl SW6	43	E3
Royal Av SW3	45	D2
Royal Coll St NW1	22	A2
Royal Cres W11	34	B2
Royal Ex EC3	32	B4
Royal Hosp Rd SW3	45	D3
Royal Ms, The SW1	37	F4
Royal Mint Ct EC3	41	D1
Royal Mint St E1	41	D1
Royal Oak Rd E8	25	F1
Royal Oak Yd SE1	40	C3
Royal Opera Arc SW1	38	B2
Royal Rd SE17	47	F3
Royal St SE1	39	D4
Rozel Ct N1	24	C3
Ruby St SE15	49	F3
Ruckholt Cl E10	50	C1
Ruckholt Rd E10	50	C2
Rudolph Rd NW6	19	E4
Rufford St N1	22	C3
Rugby St WC1	31	D2
Rumbold Rd SW6	43	F4
Runcorn Pl W11	34	C1
Rupert Rd NW6	19	D4
Rupert St W1	38	B1
Rushton St N1	24	B4
Rushworth St SE1	39	F3
Russell Gdns W14	34	C4
Russell Gdns Ms W14	34	C4
Russell Gro SW9	47	E4
Russell Rd W14	34	C4
Russell Sq WC1	30	C3
Russell St WC2	31	D4
Rust Sq SE5	48	B4
Ruston St E3	52	A2
Rutherford St SW1	46	B1
Rutland Gate SW7	36	C3
Rutland Gdns SW7	36	C3
Rutland Pk NW2	18	A1
Rutland St SW7	36	C3
Ryder Dr SE16	49	F2
Ryder St SW1	38	A2
Ryland Rd NW5	21	F1
Rylston Rd SW6	43	D3
Rysbrack St SW3	37	D4

S

Name	Page	Grid
Sabella Ct E3	52	A3
Sable St N1	23	F2
Sackville St W1	38	A1
Saffron Hill EC1	31	E2
Sail St SE11	47	D1
St. Agnes Pl SE11	47	E3
St. Albans Gro W8	35	F4
St. Alban's Pl N1	23	F3
St. Andrew's Hill EC4	39	F1
St. Andrews Pl NW1	29	F2
St. Andrews Rd W14	42	C3
St. Andrew St EC4	31	E3
St. Anns Rd W11	34	B1
St. Ann's St SW1	38	B4
St. Ann's Ter NW8	20	B4
St. Anns Vil W11	34	B2
St. Anthonys Cl E1	41	E2
St. Augustines Rd NW1	22	B2
St. Barnabas St SW1	45	E2
St. Botolph St EC3	33	D4
St. Bride St EC4	31	F4
St. Chad's Pl WC1	30	C1
St. Chad's St WC1	30	C1
St. Charles Sq W10	26	C3
St. Clements St N7	23	E1
St. Cross St EC1	31	E3
St. Cuthberts Rd NW2	19	D1
St. Dunstan's Hill EC3	40	C1
St. Dunstans Rd W6	42	B2
St. Edmunds Sq SW13	42	A3
St. Edmunds Ter NW8	20	C3
St. Ervans Rd W10	26	C3
St. Georges Circ SE1	39	F4
St. George's Dr SW1	45	F1
St. Georges Flds W2	28	C4
St. Georges Rd E10	51	D1
St. Georges Rd SE1	39	E4
St. George's Sq SW1	46	B2
St. George's Sq Ms SW1	46	B2
St. George St W1	29	F4
St. Georges Way SE15	48	C3
St. George Wf SW8	46	C2
St. Giles High St WC2	30	B4
St. Giles Rd SE5	48	C4
St. Helens Gdns W10	26	B4
St. Hildas Cl NW6	18	B2
St. James's Ct SW1	38	A4
St. James's Gdns W11	34	C2
St. James's Palace SW1	38	A2
St. James's Pk SW1	38	A3
St. James's Pl SW1	38	A2
St. James's Rd SE1	49	E2
St. James's Rd SE16	41	E4
St. James's Sq SW1	38	A2
St. James's St SW1	38	A2
St. James's Ter Ms NW8	21	D3
St. James St W6	42	A2
St. James's Wk EC1	31	F2
St. John's Est N1	24	B4
St. John's Gdns W11	35	D1
St. John's La EC1	31	F2
St. John St EC1	31	F2
St. John's Wd High St NW8	20	B4
St. John's Wd Pk NW8	20	B3
St. John's Wd Rd NW8	28	B2
St. John's Wd Ter NW8	20	B4
St. Jude's Rd E2	25	F4
St. Julian's Rd NW6	19	D2
St. Katharine's Way E1	41	D2
St. Laurence Cl NW6	18	B3
St. Lawrence Ter W10	26	C3
St. Leonards Ct N1	32	B1
St. Leonards Sq NW5	21	E1
St. Leonards St E3	52	C4
St. Leonard's Ter SW3	45	D2
St. Loo Av SW3	44	C3
St. Luke's Cl EC1	32	A2
St. Luke's Est EC1	32	B1
St. Lukes Rd W11	27	D3
St. Luke's St SW3	44	C2
St. Luke's Yd W9	19	D4
St. Margarets La W8	35	F4
St. Margaret's Rd NW10	26	A1
St. Margaret's St SW1	38	C3
St. Marks Cres NW1	21	E3
St. Mark's Gate E9	52	A1
St. Mark's Gro SW10	43	F3
St. Marks Pl W11	26	C4
St. Marks Rd W10	26	B4
St. Marks Rd W11	26	C4
St. Marks Sq NW1	21	E3
St. Mark St E1	33	D4
St. Martins Cl NW1	22	A3
St. Martin's La WC2	38	C1
St. Martin's-le-Grand EC1	32	A4
St. Martin's Pl WC2	38	C1
St. Mary Abbots Pl W8	35	D4
St. Mary Abbots Ter W14	35	D4
St. Mary at Hill EC3	40	C1
St. Mary Axe EC3	32	C4
St. Mary's Gdns SE11	47	E1
St. Mary's Gate W8	35	F4
St. Mary's Gro N1	23	F1
St. Marys Mans W2	28	A3
St. Marys Path N1	23	F3
St. Mary's Rd E10	51	D1
St. Marys Sq W2	28	B3
St. Marys Ter W2	28	B3
St. Mary's Wk SE11	47	E1
St. Matthew's Row E2	33	E1
St. Michaels St W2	28	B4
St. Olaf's Rd SW6	42	C4
St. Oswald's Pl SE11	47	D2
St. Pancras Way NW1	22	A2
St. Paul's Chyd EC4	31	F4
St. Paul's Cres NW1	22	B2
St. Paul's Drive E15	51	E3
St. Paul's Ms NW1	22	B2
St. Paul's Pl N1	24	B2
St. Paul's Rd N1	23	F1
St. Paul's Shrubbery N1	24	B1
St. Paul St N1	24	A3
St. Petersburgh Ms W2	35	F1
St. Petersburgh Pl W2	35	F1
St. Peter's Cl E2	25	E4
St. Peters St N1	23	F3
St. Peters Ter SW6	42	C4
St. Peter's Way N1	24	C2
St. Philip's Rd E8	25	F1
St. Quintin Av W10	26	A3
St. Quintin Gdns W10	26	A3
St. Saviour's Est SE1	41	D4
St. Silas Pl NW5	21	E1
St. Silas St Est NW5	21	E1
St. Stephens Cres W2	27	E4
St. Stephens Gdns W2	27	E4
St. Stephen's Rd E3	52	A3
St. Stephens Ter SW8	47	D4
St. Stephen's Wk SW7	44	A1
St. Swithin's La EC4	40	B1
St. Thomas's Sq E9	25	F2
St. Thomas St SE1	40	B2
St. Thomas's Way SW6	43	D4
Salamanca St SE1	46	C1
Sale Pl W2	28	C3
Salem Rd W2	35	F1
Salisbury Ct EC4	31	F4
Salisbury Pl SW9	47	F4
Salisbury Pl W1	29	D3
Salisbury St NW8	28	C2
Salters Rd W10	26	B2
Saltram Cres W9	27	D3
Salusbury Rd NW6	18	C3
Salway Pl E15	51	F4
Salway Rd E15	51	E4
Samford St NW8	28	C2
Sampson St E1	41	E2
Samuel Lewis Trust Dws SW6	43	E4
Samuel St SE15	49	D4
Sancroft St SE11	47	D2
Sandal St E15	53	F2
Sandall Rd NW5	22	A1
Sandgate St SE15	49	F3
Sandland St WC1	31	D3
Sandwell Cres NW6	19	E1
Sandwich St WC1	30	C1
Sandy's Row E1	32	C3

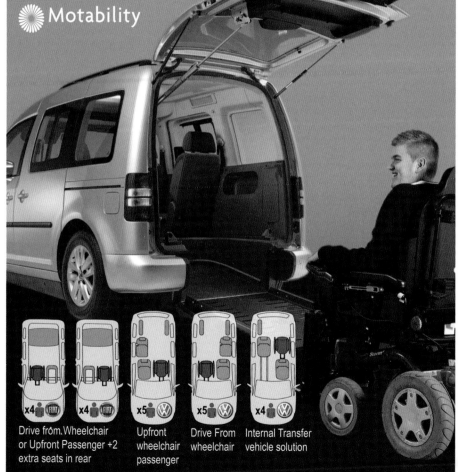

Welcome!

I am delighted that the Society of London Theatre is once again collaborating with the Blue Badge Parking Guide for London in 2012, the year of the London Paralympics.

In this guide you can find out the exact location of the nearest Blue Badge parking space to over 70 theatres in the West End and across London. We've also provided you with detailed venue access information including the location of lifts and ramps, information on where disabled toilets are situated, how many steps there are in each venue and whether the theatre offers sound amplification. You'll also find useful contact details if you would like to find out more information about the theatre or book tickets.

I hope you find the guide useful and enjoy many wonderful nights out at the theatre.

Mark Rubinstein
President

The Society of London Theatre
32 Rose Street
London
WC2E 9ET

If you have any access queries, please contact the Society of London Theatre at the above address, call 020 7557 6700 or email **enquiries@solttma.co.uk**

For further online information on access in London theatres, please visit the Society's website **www.officiallondontheatre.co.uk/access** where you can sign-up to a monthly access bulletin, view detailed information on venue facilities and find details of assisted performances taking place.

Theatre accessibility information

To ensure a pleasant experience visiting the theatre, booking in advance and informing the theatre of your requirements is recommended. Some theatres offer transfer seating for those able to transfer from their chair or spaces for wheelchairs at end of rows allowing you to sit next to non-disabled companions.

The new theatre directory lists the theatres in and around London and is cross referenced to the map pages and the grid square they are located in for your convenience.

These numbered locations appear as 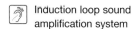 on the maps and in the directory.

In most venues, staff will bring drinks to disabled customers during the interval.

Symbols used in the directory

Theatre operates a sound amplification system

 Induction loop sound amplification system

 Sennheiser infrared sound amplification system

Access from street to foyer, if there isn't a symbol assume level access

 Steps   Ramp   Lift

For further information on theatre accessibility, transport and assisted performances please consult **www.officiallondontheatre.co.uk/access** or email **enquiries@solttma.co.uk**

ENJOY LONDON THEATRE

AUDIO-DESCRIBED, **CAPTIONED** and **SIGN LANGUAGE INTERPRETED** performances are making theatre more accessible and enjoyable.

Call **020 7557 6700** or email **enquiries@solttma.co.uk** for a free brochure listing assisted performances, available in large print, Braille or on tape.

You can also sign up to receive a monthly bulletin packed full of theatre access news at
www.officiallondontheatre.co.uk/access

Name	No.	Page/Ref	Address	Telephone number	Email or fax or minicom / typetalk
Adelphi	1	38 C1	Strand, WC2E 7NA	0844 412 4648	customer.relations@seetickets.com
Aldwych	2	31 D4	Aldwych, WC2B 4DF	020 7836 5537	access@aldwychtheatre.co.uk
Almeida	3	23 F3	Almeida Street, N1 1TA	020 7288 4999	access@almeida.co.uk
Ambassadors	4	30 B4	West Street, WC2H 9ND	020 7395 5405	access@theambassadorstheatre.co.uk
Apollo	5	38 B1	Shaftesbury Avenue, W1D 7EZ	0844 412 4648	www.nimaxtheatres.com
Apollo Victoria	6	46 A1	Wilton Street, SW1V 1LG	020 7828 7074	apollovic.bookings@livenation.co.uk
Arts	7	38 C1	Great Newport Street, WC2H 7JB	020 7240 7327	boxoffice@artstheatrelondon.com
Barbican (including The Pit)	8	32 A3	Silk Street, EC2Y 8DS	0845 120 7511	Minicom 020 7382 7297 access@barbican.org.uk
Cambridge	9	30 C4	Earlham Street, WC2H 9HU	020 7087 7777	customer.relations@seetickets.com
Dominion	10	30 B4	Tottenham Court Road, W1T 7AQ	020 7927 0929	
Donmar Warehouse	11	30 C4	Earlham Street, WC2H 9LX	020 7845 5813	donmarmanager@theambassadors.com
Drill Hall	12	30 B3	Chenies Street, WC1E 7EX	020 7307 5060	box.office@drillhall.co.uk
Drury Lane, Theatre Royal	13	31 D4	Catherine Street, WC2B 5JF	0844 412 4648	customer.relations@seetickets.com
Duchess	14	39 D1	Catherine Street, WC2B 5LA	0844 482 9677	access@nimaxtheatres.com
Duke of York's	15	38 C1	St Martin's Lane, WC2N 4BG	0870 060 6623	doyboxoffice@theambassadors.com
Fortune	16	30 C4	Russell Street, WC2B 5HH	0870 060 6626	fortuneboxoffice@theambassadors.com

disabled toilets situated	number of wheelchair spaces	sound amplification	access from street to foyer	Access from theatre foyer to seats		
				Steps	Level Access	Stairlift / Lift / Ramp available
Stalls Foyer	Stalls x2		[ramp]	41 to Dress Circle / 79 to Upper Circle	to Stalls	
Circle	Circle x4	[ear]	[ramp]	15 to back of Dress Circle. 26 to Stalls / 50+ to Grand Circle	to Front of Dress Circle	
Foyer	Stalls x4	[ear] [ear]	[ramp]	54 steps to Circle		Sloped walkway to Stalls
		[ear]	[steps]	26 to Stalls / 5 to Circle		
Stalls	Stalls x2	[ear]	[steps]	21 to Stalls / 12 to Dress Circle / 35 to Upper Circle / 75 to balcony		to Stalls
Foyer	Circle x4	[ear] [ear]	[steps] [wheelchair]	29 to Stalls / 13 to Circle		to Circle
Circle	Circle x2		[ramp]	5 to Circle / 19 to Stalls		Ramp from street to Dress Circle
Stalls Circle Foyer	Stalls x4 Circle x4	[ear]		28 to Stalls / 27 to Circle / 21 to Upper Circle / 15 to Gallery	Row T Stalls Row B Circle	Lifts to all floors
Stalls	Stalls x2	[ear]	[ramp]	4 to Stalls / 31 to Dress Circle / 64 Upper Circle		
Stalls	Stalls x4	[ear]	[ramp]	9 to Stalls / 18+ to Circle	Yes	Yes
Circle	Stalls x1	[ear]	[steps] [ramp]			Yes
Foyer	Stalls x4	[ear]	[ramp]		Drill Hall 1	Drill Hall 2 by lift
Stalls	Stalls x4	[ear] [ear]	[steps]	20 down then 17 up to Stalls / 39 to Dress Circle / 61 to Upper Circle	to Stalls	
Stalls	Stalls x2	[ear]	[steps]	20 to Stalls / 10 to Dress Circle		AAT Stairclimber to Stalls
Circle	Circle x2			23 Stalls / 23 Upper Circle	Royal Circle Row D (wheelchair spaces)	
		[ear] [ear]		21 Stallls / 7 Dress / 40 Upper Circle		

Name	No.	Page/Ref	Address	Telephone number	Email or fax or minicom / typetalk
Garrick	17	38 C1	Charing Cross Road, WC2H 0HH	0844 412 4648	customer.relations@seetickets.com
Gate	18	35 E2	Pembridge Road, Notting Hill Gate, W11 3HQ	020 7229 0706	gate@gatetheatre.co.uk
Gielgud	19	38 B1	Shaftesbury Avenue, W1D 6AR	0844 482 5137	access@delmack.co.uk
Greenwich Playhouse	20	off map	Greenwich High Rd, SE10 8JA	020 8858 9256	box office@galleontheatre.co.uk
Greenwich Theatre	21	off map	Crooms Hill, SE10 8ES	020 8858 7755	boxoffice@greenwichtheatre.org.uk
Hackney Empire	22	25 F1	291 Mare Street, E8 1EJ	020 8510 4500	frank.sweeny@hackneyempire.co.uk
Hampstead and Hampstead Downstairs	23	off map	Eton Avenue, NW3 3EU	020 7722 9301	access@hampsteadtheatre.com
Harold Pinter	24	38 B1	Panton Street, SW1Y 4DN	0871 2975 477	ticketcentre@theambassadors.com
Her Majesty's	25	38 B2	Haymarket, SW1Y 4QL	0844 412 2707	customer.relations@seetickets.com
Leicester Square Theatre	26	38 B1	6 Leicester Place, WC2H 7BP	020 7534 1740	boxoffice@leicestersquaretheatre.com
London Coliseum - ENO	27	38 C1	St. Martin's Lane, WC2N 4ES	0871 9112244	access@eno.org
London Palladium	28	30 A4	Argyll Street, W1F 7TF	020 7087 7960	customer.relations@seetickets.com
Lyceum Theatre	29	39 D1	Wellington Street, WC2E 7RQ	020 7420 8113	
Lyric - Hammersmith	30	42 A1	King Street, W6 0QL	0871 221 1722	enquiries@lyric.co.uk
Lyric - Shaftesbury Avenue	31	38 B1	Shaftesbury Avenue, W1D 7ES	0844 412 4648	access@nimaxtheatres.com
National - Cottesloe, Lyttelton & Olivier	32	39 D2	South Bank, SE1 9PX	020 7452 3000 020 7452 3400	boxoffice@nationaltheatre.org.uk access@nationaltheatre.org.uk www.nationaltheatre.org.uk/access

disabled toilets situated	number of wheelchair spaces	sound amplification	access from street to foyer	Access from theatre foyer to seats Steps	Level Access	Stairlift / Lift / Ramp available
Foyer	**Circle** x2	[hearing icon]	[ramp icon]		Dress Circle	
Foyer		[hearing icon]	[steps icon]	8 to stalls		
Foyer	**Circle** x2	[hearing icon] [hearing icon]	[steps icon] [ramp icon]	20 to Stalls 30 Grand Circle		
No information available						
Foyer	**Circle** x2	[hearing icon]	[ramp icon]	3 flights of stairs		Lift to auditorium
Stalls **Circle** Foyer	Stalls x10 **Circle** x12	[hearing icon] [hearing icon]			Stalls	Lift to Dress, Upper & Gallery
Stalls **Circle** Foyer	Stalls x4 **Downstairs** x2	[hearing icon] [hearing icon]			Yes	Yes
Foyer	**Circle** x4		[steps icon] [ramp icon]		Yes	
Stalls	Stalls x4	[hearing icon]	[ramp icon]	18 Stalls 32 Royal Circle 62 Grand Circle 89 Balcony	Yes (to Stalls)	
	Stalls x1		[steps icon]	8 to auditorium		Baronmead Stair-climber available - 24 hours notice needed
Stalls **Circle** Balcony	Stalls x8 **Circle** x2	[hearing icon] [hearing icon]	[ramp icon]			Lift to all auditorium levels
Stalls	Stalls x4	[hearing icon] [hearing icon]	[ramp icon]	26+ Royal Circle 47+ Upper Circle		Lift from Street to Stalls
Stalls	Stalls x8	[hearing icon] [hearing icon]	[ramp icon]	82 Grand Circle	Stalls	Lift to Royal or Grand Circle
Stalls Foyer	Stalls x4 - Main Theatre x9 in Studio	[hearing icon] [hearing icon]	[ramp icon] [wheelchair icon]	33 Stalls 26 Circle 26 Upper Circle		Lift to get to all levels
Foyer	**Circle** x4	[hearing icon]	[ramp icon]	23 to Stalls 25 to Upper Circle & 60 to balcony	Dress Circle Boxes C, D & E	
Foyer	**Stalls** x5 in Olivier x4 in Lyttelton x2 in Cottesloe	[hearing icon]		1 to Olivier	Lyttelton & Cottesloe from from back of Stalls	Lift and ramps to all levels

Name	No.	Page/ Ref	Address	Telephone number	Email or fax or minicom / typetalk
New End	33		27 New End, Hampstead, NW3 1JD	0870 033 2733	020 7794 4044
New London	34	30 C4	Drury Lane, WC2B 5PW	0844 412 4648	customer.relations@seetickets.com
New Wimbledon	35	*off map*	The Broadway, SW19 1QG	0844 871 7677	wimbledonboxoffice@theambassadors.com
Noel Coward (Albery)	36	38 C1	St Martin's Lane, WC2N 4AA	0844 482 5137	access@delmack.co.uk
Novello (Strand)	37	39 D1	Aldwych, WC2B 4LD	0844 482 5137	access@delmack.co.uk
Old Red Lion	38	23 F4	418 St John Street, EC1V 4NJ	020 7837 7816	
Old Vic	39	39 E3	Waterloo Road, SE1 8NB	0844 871 7677	18001 0844 871 7628 (text phone users)
Orange Tree	40	*off map*	Clarence Street, Richmond, TW9 2SA	020 8940 3633	
Oval House	41	47 D3	Kennington Oval, SE11 5SW	020 7582 7680	info@ovalhouse.com
Palace	42	30 B4	Shaftesbury Avenue, W1D 5AY	0844 412 4648	customer.relations@seetickets.com Fax: 020 7087 7771 Minicom: 020 7087 7839
Peacock	43	31 D4	Portugal Street, WC2A 2HT	0844 412 4322	ticket.office@sadlerswells.com Minicom: 020 7863 8015
Phoenix	44	30 B4	Charing Cross Road, WC2H 0JP	0844 871 7677	phoenixboxoffice@theambassadors.com
Piccadilly	45	38 B1	Denman Street, W1D 7DY	0844 871 7677	piccadillyboxoffice@theambassadors.com
Playhouse	46	38 C2	Northumberland Avenue, WC2N 5DE	0844 871 7677	ticketcentre@theambassadors.com

disabled toilets situated	number of wheelchair spaces	sound amplification	access from street to foyer	Access from theatre foyer to seats Steps	Level Access	Stairlift / Lift / Ramp available
Foyer	Stalls x2		[stairs] [ramp]		Yes	
Foyer Stalls	Stalls x2	[hearing]	[ramp]	65 to Dress Circle Escalator plus 30 Steps to Stalls		Lift to Stalls
Foyer	Stalls x8 in Main Theatre Unrestricted in Studio	[hearing]	[stairs]			Lift from Street level to Stalls
Foyer	Stalls x2	[hearing]	[ramp]	30 to Stalls 30 to Grand Circle 40 to Balcony	Box M & L	Ramp to Royal Circle
Circle	Circle x2	[hearing]	[stairs]	20 to Stalls 10 to Dress Circle		Chair lift from Catherine Street to Circle
Stalls	Stalls x1 2 transfer spaces	[hearing]	[stairs]	3 to Stalls 29 to Dress Circle 20 to Bayliss		
Foyer	Stalls x2	[hearing] [hearing]	[ramp]			Ramp
Foyer	Downstairs Theatre x5	[hearing]	[ramp]		Stalls	
Stalls	Stalls x3	[hearing]	[stairs]	23 Stalls from foyer 30 to Dress Circle 26 Dress Circle to Grand Circle 21 Grand Circle to Balcony	Stalls	
Foyer	Circle x2 Stalls x2	[hearing]	[ramp]			Ramp/Lift from Street level to foyer & foyer to auditorium
Circle	Circle x1	[hearing] [hearing]	[stairs]	24 to Stalls 21 to Dress Circle 42 to Upper Circle		
Foyer	Circle x2	[hearing]	[stairs] [ramp]	15 to Stalls 30 to Royal Circle 70 to Grand Circle		
Foyer	Stalls x2	[hearing] [hearing]	[ramp]	28 to Dress Circle 82 to Upper Circle	Yes (Stalls)	

Name	No.	Page/Ref	Address	Telephone number	Email or fax or minicom / typetalk
Polka	47	off map	The Broadway, SW19 1SB	020 8543 4888	kim@polkatheatre.com
Prince Edward	48	30 B4	Old Compton Street, W1D 4HS	020 7447 5459	petbox@delfont-mackintosh.com
Prince of Wales	49	38 B1	Coventry Street, W1D 6AS	0844 482 5137 0844 482 5115	paccess@delfont-mackintosh.com
Queen's	50	38 B1	Shaftesbury Avenue, W1D 6BA	0844 482 5137	access@queens-theatre.co.uk
Regent's Park Open Air	51	29 E1	Inner Circle Regents Park, NW1 4NR	0844 826 4242	boxoffice@openairtheatre.com
Richmond Theatre	52	off map	The Little Green, Richmond, TW9 1QJ	0870 060 6651	richmondboxoffice@theambassadors.com
Riverside Studios	53	42 A2	Crisp Road, W6 9RL	020 8237 1111	online@riversidestudios.co.uk
Roundhouse	54	21 E2	Chalk Farm Road, NW1 8EH	0844 482 8008	boxoffice@roundhouse.org.uk
Royal Albert Hall	55	36 B3	Kensington Gore, SW7 2AP	020 7838 3110	BoxOfficeEnquiries@royalalberthall.com
Royal Court	56	45 E1	Sloane Square, SW1W 8AS	020 7565 5000	access@royalcourttheatre.com
Royal Festival Hall	57	39 D2	Belvedere Road, SE1 8XX	0871 663 2500	0871 663 2594
Royal Opera House	58	30 C4	Covent Garden, WC2E 9DD	020 7304 4000	Fax 020 7212 9460 boxofficeaccess@roh.org.uk
Sadler's Wells	59	31 E1	Rosebery Avenue, EC1R 4TN	0844 412 4300	Minicom 020 7863 8015 ticket.office@sadlerswells.com
Savoy	60	39 D1	The Strand, WC2R 0ET	0844 871 7677	savoyboxoffice@theambassadors.com
Shaftesbury / Theatre of Comedy	61	30 C4	Shaftesbury Avenue, WC2H 8DP	020 7379 5399	Fax 020 7836 0466

disabled toilets situated	number of wheelchair spaces	sound amplification	access from street to foyer	Access from theatre foyer to seats		Stairlift / Lift / Ramp available
				Steps	Level Access	
Foyer	Stalls x6 in Main Theatre x2 in Adventure Theatre	[hearing]	[ramp]			Lift
Foyer	Stalls x2 (Box 1)	[hearing]	[ramp]	22 to Stalls 13 to Dress Circle 42 to Grand Circle (front) 72 to Grand Circle (back)	Yes (to Box 1)	
Foyer	Stalls x3	[hearing]	[ramp]	70 to Dress Circle	Yes (Stalls)	
Foyer	Stalls x2 **Circle** x4	[hearing] [hearing]	[steps]	18 to Stalls 19 to Dress Circle 38 to Upper Circle	Yes (to Box Office)	
Foyer	Stalls x20	[hearing]	[ramp]		Yes	
Stalls	Stalls x4	[hearing] [hearing]	[ramp]		Yes (Stalls)	
Stalls Foyer	Stalls x3				Yes	
Stalls **Circle** Foyer	Stalls x8 **Circle** x4	[hearing] [hearing]	[steps] [ramp]	8 to Stalls	Yes	Yes
Foyer	Stalls x12 **Circle** x6	[hearing] [hearing]	[steps] [ramp] [wheelchair]	5 to Loggia Boxes		Lifts to Grand Tier, Second Tier, Circle and Gallery
Foyer	Stalls x5	[hearing] [hearing]	[ramp]			Lift to auditoriums
Stalls **Circle** Foyer	Stalls x19 **Circle** x19	[hearing]	[steps] [ramp] [wheelchair]		Yes	Yes
All levels	Stalls x19 **Circle** x19	[hearing]	[wheelchair]		Yes	Yes
Stalls **Circle**	Stalls x3 **Circle** x1	[hearing]	[ramp]			Lifts to all levels
Royal Circle	**Circle** x4		[steps] [ramp]	75 to Stalls 32 to Dress Circle 2 to Upper Circle	Yes (Dress Circle)	Ramp
Circle	Stalls x4	[hearing]	[ramp]		Yes (Royal Circle)	

Name	No.	Page/Ref	Address	Telephone number	Email or fax or minicom / typetalk
Shakespeare's Globe	62	40 A1	New Globe Walk, SE1 9DT	020 7902 1409	access@shakespearesglobe.com
Shaw	63	30 B1	Euston Road, NW1 2AJ	0844 248 5075	info@shaw-theatre.com www@shaw-theatre.com
Soho	64	30 B4	21 Dean Street, W1D 3NE	020 7478 0100	box1@sohotheatre.com
Southwark Playhouse	65	40 A3	Tooley Street/ Bermondsey Street, SE1 0AS	0844 847 1656	www.southwarkplayhouse.co.uk
St Martin's	66	38 C1	West Street, WC2H 9NZ	020 7395 5408	access@stmartinstheatre.co.uk
Theatre Royal, Haymarket	67	38 B1	Suffolk Street, SW1Y 4HT	020 7930 8800	tix@trh.co.uk
Trafalgar Studios	68	38 C2	Whitehall, SW1A 2DY	0844 8717 677	trafalgarboxoffice@theambassadors.com
Tricycle	69	19 D2	Kilburn High Road, NW6 7JR	020 7328 1000	boxofficemanager@tricycle.co.uk
UCL Bloomsbury	70	30 B2	Gower Street, WC1H 0AH	020 7679 2915	g.cummings@ucl.ac.uk
Unicorn	71	40 C2	Tooley Street, SE1 2HZ	020 7645 0560	boxoffice@unicorntheatre.com
Vaudeville	72	38 B1	Strand, WC2R 0NH	0844 482 9677	access@nimaxtheatres.com
Victoria Palace	73	38 A4	Victoria Street, SW1E 5EA	020 7834 1170	access@victoriapalace.co.uk
Warehouse Theatre	74	94	Dingwall Road, Croydon, CR0 2NF	0208 6804060	020 8688 6699
Wyndham's	75	38 C1	Charing Cross Road, WC2H 0DA	0844 482 5160	wyndhamsbox@delfont-mackintosh.com
Young Vic	76	39 E3	The Cut, SE1 8LZ	020 7922 2922	info@youngvic.org

disabled toilets situated	number of wheelchair spaces	sound amplification	access from street to foyer	Access from theatre foyer to seats Steps	Level Access	Stairlift / Lift / Ramp available
Stalls **Circle** Foyer	Stalls x1 **Circle** x3	[hearing]	[ramp]		Yes	Ramp to Stalls Lift to Circle
Foyer	Stalls x5		[ramp]		Yes (Row A only)	
Upstairs **Theatre** Foyer	Upstairs x3+ **Main House** x2+ Downstairs x3+	[hearing]	Level access	36 to 1st Floor 17 more to Upstairs 21 down to Downstairs		Lift to all floors
Foyer	Stalls x2		[stairlift] [ramp]		Yes	
Circle	Circle x2	[hearing]	[stairlift]	20+ to Stalls 5 to Dress Circle		Box C and Dress Circle via ramp
Stalls	Stalls x2	[hearing]	[stairlift]	28 up to Royal Circle 60+ to Upper Circle and Gallery		
	Stalls x2 **Circle** x2		[stairlift]	14 up to Studio 1 28 down to Studio 2		
Foyer	Circle x2	[hearing]	[ramp]	7 steps to Royal Circle		Yes
Foyer	Stalls x2	[hearing]		15 down to Lower Ground 7 to Stalls 28 + to Dress Circle		Yes
Stalls **Circle** Foyer	Stalls x23	[hearing]	[stairlift] [ramp]	22 down to Lower Ground 57 up to Weston Level to Clore Studio	Yes	Lift to all floors
			[stairlift]	6 down to Stalls 27 up to Dress Circle 54 up to Upper Circle		AAT Stairclimber to Stalls
Stalls	Stalls x2	[hearing] [hearing]		4 down to Stalls 28 to Dress Circle		
Foyer		[hearing]		20 to studio		
	Stalls x2	[hearing]	[stairlift]	21 down to Stalls 23 to Royal Circle 40 to Grand		
Balcony Foyer	Varies with configuration Min 2	[hearing]			Yes	Yes

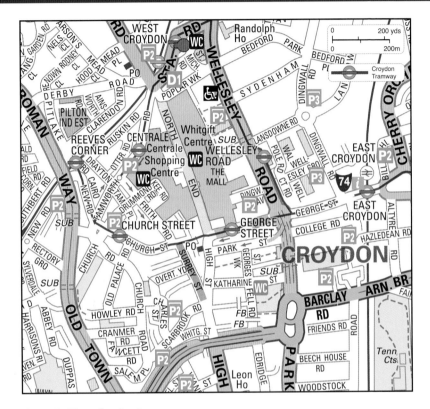

Centrale Shopping Centre

Address: 21 North End, CR0 1TY Tel: **0208 681 5841**   Sat Nav: CR0 1XT

Parking - Car park is situated in Tamworth Road with wheelchair accessible on all levels. Accessible toilets located on the Upper Mall, North End Mall and Lower Mall.

The Whitgift Centre

Address: Croydon, CR0 1LP Tel: **020 8688 8522**   Sat Nav: CR0 1UP

Parking - Multi-storey car park situated in Wellesley Road with 35 disabled spaces and a height restriction of 1.90m

Shopmobility - scheme offers wheelchair hire. Tel: 0208 688 7336.
Disabled Toilets located on Level 3, Whitgift Square and Level 2, Sainsbury's Square.

Council Parking Enquiries: Tel: **020 8726 7100** email: **parking@croydon.gov.uk**

Address: PO Box 1462, Croydon, CR9 1NX

Kingston upon Thames

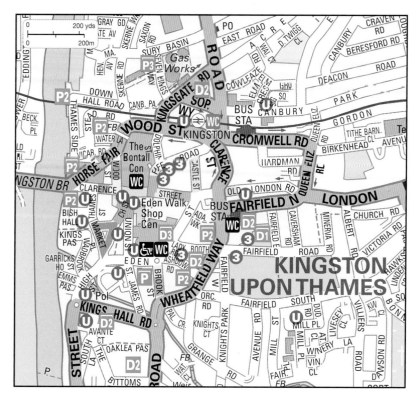

The Bentall Centre

Address: Wood Street, KT1 1TP Tel: **0208 541 5066** (option 4).
Parking - Kings Car Park. Off Sury Basin with 35 bays dedicated for disabled users.
Disabled toilets are on the ground floor.　　　　　　　Sat Nav: KT2 5AD
Alternatively Car Park B　　　　　　　　　　　　　　Sat Nav: KT1 1TY
Disabled toilet facilities located on 2nd floor. Radar Key required or member of
security or cleaning team will give access. Three separate disabled toilets offer a
variety of amenities including: bench, hoist for adult changing and ambulant
cubicles located in the male and female toilets.

Eden Walk Shopping Centre

Address: Eden Street, KT1 1BL Tel: **020 8549 9672**
Disabled toilets are situated near Eden Walk entrance.
Shopmobility - Wheelchair hire is situated at the Eden Walk car park in Union Street.
Tel: **020 8547 1255.**
Council Parking Enquiries: Tel: **020 8547 5002**
Address: Guildhall 2, High Street, Kingston upon Thames, KT1 1EU

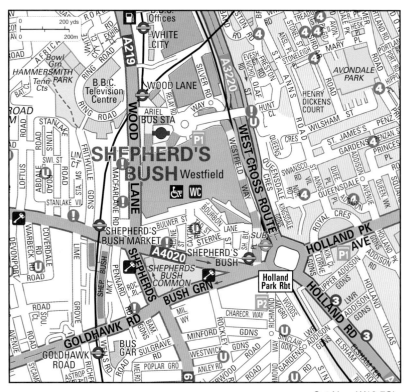

Sat Nav: W12 7SL

Westfield Shopping Centre

Parking

There is vehicle height restriction of 2.20m in the Shopmobility car park area. If your vehicle is over this height, call the booking number below and staff will advise you on alternative parking.

Shopmobility

The desk is located within lift lobby 2 (Middle car park) adjacent to the Ariel Way roundabout. You can book a wheelchair or motorised scooter including 4 hours free parking on weekdays.

Manual wheelchairs are available on the day, but motorised scooters and wheelchairs need to be booked in advance and are subject to a time limit of 4 hours (this can be extended on request). To book you will need proof of identification and call **020 3371 2402**.

Council Parking Enquiries: Tel: **020 7371 5678**

Address: Hammersmith & Fulham Council, Town Hall, King St., Hammersmith, W6 9JU

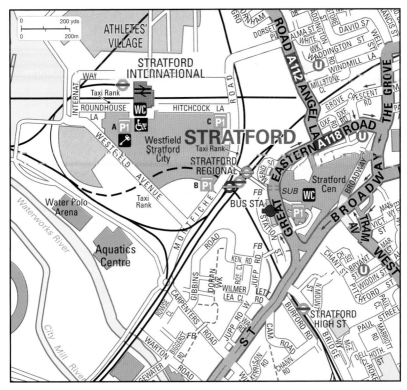

Sat Nav: E15 2JU

Westfield Shopping Centre

Parking

Designated parking bays for people with disabilities are available in each car park. The northern taxi rank, located near Stratford International station is frequently used by wheelchair users as it is located closest to the step free access into shopmobility and the shopping centre.

Shopmobility

The Shopmobility desk is located at street level (or lower ground within the mall) beneath car park A and adjacent to the taxi rank. Shopmobility hire out manual wheelchairs and electric scooters to use within Westfield Stratford City.

The height restriction within the car parks is 2.2m. High-sided vehicles up to 2.4m for blue badge holders are catered for in the Lower Ground Floor car park A, the location of the Shopmobility facility.

Council Parking Enquiries: Tel: **020 8430 2000** Textphone: **020 8430 2412**

Address: Newham Dockside, 1000 Dockside Rd., E16 2QU

Shopmobility

National Federation of Shopmobility UK
Tel: **0845 644 2446**
Email: **info@shopmobilityuk.org**
www.shopmobilityuk.org

Shopmobility is a scheme which lends wheelchairs, powered wheelchairs and scooters to members of the public with limited mobility to enable them to shop and to visit leisure and commercial facilities within the town, city or shopping centre. Each Shopmobility centre varies so it is important to contact them in advance to find out what assistance is available. The name, location and contact details for the Shopmobility centres in and around London are:

Scheme Location	Contact Number	Address	Town/County	Postcode
Barking & Dagenham	020 8252 5340	51, Ripple Road	Essex	IG11 7NT
Beckenham (B.A.T.H)	020 8663 3345	Lewis House, 30 Beckenham Road	Beckenham	BR3 4LS
Bexley Heath	020 8301 5237	Broadway Shopping Centre	Bexley Heath	DA6 7JJ
Brent Cross	020 8457 4070	Brent Cross Shopping Centre	Hendon	NW4 3FP
Bromley	020 8313 0031	The Glades Shopping Centre Car Park	Bromley	BR1 1DN
Camden*	020 7482 5503	29a, Pratt Street, Camden	Camden	NW1 0BG
Croydon*	020 8688 7336	Whitgift Car Park	Croydon	CR0 2AG
Ealing	020 8579 1724	Arcadia Centre, The Broadway	Ealing	W5 2NH
Edmonton	020 8379 1193	4, Monmouth Road	Edmonton	N9 0LS
Hammersmith & Fulham	020 3371 2402	Westfield Shopping Centre, Shepherd's Bush	Shepherd's Bush	W12 7GF
Harrow	020 8427 1200	37, St Georges Centre	Harrow	HA1 1HS
Haringey	020 8275 2444	Mobile unit - ring for details	Haringey	E8 4RH
Hillingdon (Uxbridge)	01895 271 510	Chimes Shopping Centre, High Street	Uxbridge	UB8 1GD
Hounslow	020 8570 3343	Blenheim Centre, Prince Regent Road	Hounslow	TW3 1NL
Ilford (Redbridge)	020 8478 6864	The Exchange Mall	Ilford	IG1 1RS
Kensington & Chelsea	020 8960 8774	Mobile unit - ring for details	Kensington	W10 5YG
Kingston upon Thames*	020 8547 1255	Eden Walk Car Park, Union Street	Kingston upon Thames	KT1 1BL
Lewisham Centre	020 8297 2735	29, Molesworth Street	Lewisham	SE13 7EP
Merton	020 8348 1001	Justin Plaza, 341 London Road	Mitcham	CR4 4BE
Newham	020 3371 2402	Westfield Shopping Centre, Stratford City	Stratford	E20 1EJ
Romford	01708 765 764	Library Shopping Mall, South Mall	Romford	RM1 3RL
Staines	01784 459 416	Two Rivers Retail Park	Staines	TW18 4WB
Sutton	020 8770 0691	St Nicholas Centre Car Park, St Nicholas Way	Sutton	SM1 1AY
Waltham Forest	020 8520 3366	Selborne Walk Shopping Centre	Waltham Forest	E17 7JR
Wandsworth	020 8875 9585	45, Garratt Lane	Wandsworth	SW18 4AD

* Shopmobility centres located on main map or shopping centre page views

For a full list of all the Shopmobility centres in the UK visit the website or email for a booklet. This publication will be available at most Shopmobility centres.

NOTE Always check local restrictions displayed on signs, pay & display machines and street markings for any variations Councils	**Blue Badge Park FREE** with no time restrictions (In some areas of the borough exemptions to the maximum stay time shown may exist)	**Pay & Display** Park FREE with no time restrictions during the enforced time period
Barking and Dagenham	✔	✔
Barnet	✔	✔
Bexley	✔	✔
Brent	✔	✔
Bromley	✔	✔
Camden (Green Badge Area)	✔	✘ 1 hr free once payment made
Camden (Not Green Badge Area)	✔	✔
Corporation of London	✔ max stay 3hrs Mon to Fri	✘ 1 hr free once payment made
Croydon	✔	✔
Ealing	✔	✔ 3 hrs
Enfield	✔	✔
Greenwich	✔	✔
Hackney	✔	✔ maximum stay restrictions apply
Hammersmith & Fulham	✔	✔
Haringey	✔	✔
Harrow	✔	✔
Havering	✔	✔
Hillingdon	✔	✔
Hounslow	✔	✔
Islington	✔	✔
Kensington and Chelsea	✔ max stay 4 hrs Mon to Fri	✘ 1 hr free once payment made
Royal Borough of Kingston upon Thames	✔	✔
Lambeth	✔	✔
Lewisham	✔	✔
Merton	✔	✔
Newham	✔	✔
Redbridge	✔	✔
Richmond	✔	✔
Southwark	✔	✔
Sutton	✔	✔
Tower Hamlets	✔	✔
Waltham Forest	✔ max stay 3 hrs	✔
Wandsworth	✔	✔
Westminster	✔ max stay 4hrs Mon to Fri	✘ 1 hr free once payment made

Key to on street parking concessions for Blue Badge holders

Free parking on Single & Double Yellow lines (3hrs max) except where un/loading restrictions apply, Pay & Display, Shared Used, Residents & Blue Badge bays

Free parking in most places (single/double yellow line, Pay & Display) except Residents Parking Bays & where un/loading restrictions apply

Shared Use Bays (Pay & Display and Resident) Park FREE with no time restrictions during the enforced time period	Resident Bays Park with no time restrictions during the enforced time period	Single & Double Yellow Lines Park for a max. 3 hrs on a Single or Double Yellow Line during the enforced time	Council Specific Contact No. For the Blue Badge Scheme
✔	✔ max stay 4 hrs	✔	020 8215 3005
✔	✔	✔	020 8359 4131
✔	✔	✔	020 8303 7777
✔	✔	✔	020 8937 4665
✔ parking in shared use bays is governed by P&D restrictions	✘	✔	020 8461 7629
✘	✘	✘	020 7974 4646
✔	✔	✔	020 7974 4646
n/a	✘	✘	020 7332 1548
✔	n/a	✔	020 8760 1966
✔ 3 hrs	✔	✔	020 8825 8000
✔	✔	✔	020 8379 6406
✔	✘	✔	020 8921 2388
✔	✘	✔	020 8356 8877
✔	n/a	✔	0845 8031 020
✔	✔	✔	020 8489 1879
✔	✔	✔	020 8424 1352
n/a	✔	✔	01708 432 797
✔	✔	✔	01895 250 123
✔	✘	✔	020 8583 3073
✔	✔	✔	020 7527 1358
✘	✘	✘	020 7361 2390
✔	✔	✔	020 8547 6600
✔	✔	✔	020 7926 6000
✔	✘	✔	020 8314 9844
✔	✔	✔	020 8545 4656
✔	✔	✔	020 8430 2000
✔	✘	✔	020 8708 3636
✔	✔	✔	020 8831 6096
✔	✘	✔	0870 600 6768
n/a	✘	✔	020 8770 5341
✔	✘	✔	020 7364 5003
✔	✔	✔	0800 882 200
✔	✔	✔	020 8871 7709
✘ 1 hr free once payment made	✘	✘	020 7823 4567

Free parking in Blue Badge Bays with limited concessions on Pay & Display

Congestion Charge for Blue Badge holders

Blue Badge holders are eligible for a 100% discount from the daily Congestion Charge.

Once registered with Transport for London (TfL), Blue Badge holders from throughout the EU do not need to pay the Congestion Charge for entering the zone during charging hours, subject to an initial £10 registration fee.

You can register up to two vehicles that you use to travel into central London. This can be your own vehicle, or a vehicle that you often travel in.

The discount applies to the person who is the Blue Badge holder, not the vehicle that is being used.

Please note that you **MUST** register the vehicle that you wish to travel in with TfL by midnight on the day of travel if it is different to the vehicles you nominated at the time of registering. If you are unable to or fail to nominate the vehicle you are travelling in on the day of travel you can pay the Congestion Charge the next day, but you will pay £12 (rather than the daily £10 charge). If you do not nominate a vehicle or pay the congestion charge by midnight the next charging day after travelling in the zone, the registered keeper of the vehicle will receive a Penalty Charge Notice.

There are instructions on how to nominate long term use and short term use vehicles, details of which are explained on TfL's Blue Badge registration form, which you can obtain in the following ways:

For more information and to download an application form for the Blue Badge 100% discount, please visit:

www.cclondon.com, click on 'Discounts and Exemptions' and then 'Blue Badge holders'

Alternatively, visit: **www.tfl.gov.uk/assets/downloads/ blue-badge-discount-registration-form.pdf**

Write to: Congestion Charging, PO Box 4782, Worthing BN11 9PS

Telephone: **0845 900 1234** or from outside the UK **+44 20 7649 9122**

Text phone: **020 7649 9123**

Please note the Congestion Charge boundary is shown in its entirety on page 14 and also appears on the relevant street map pages as a red tinted band (as on example above).

Congestion Charging Operating Hours: Monday to Friday 7am - 6pm, excluding Public Holidays and between 25th December and 1st January inclusive.

The normal daily charge is £10 which has to be paid by midnight on the day of travel. You can also pay by midnight the next charging day, but the charge will be £12.

Traffic signs and markings on the road should make it clear exactly where the charging zone is.

Congestion charging

Central ZONE

Mon - Fri
7 am - 6 pm

Save. Fuel.
Stop. More.

New Thinking. New Possibilities: getting stuck in traffic uses up a lot of fuel. So our Intelligent Stop & Go turns the engine off when you stop, and back on when you move. It's one of our Blue Drive technologies designed to reduce CO_2 emissions and fuel consumption. **To find out about all our Motability offers, visit hyundai.co.uk/motability**

5 YEAR TRIPLE CARE™
UNLIMITED MILEAGE WARRANTY

Motability
The leading car scheme for disabled people

Fuel consumption in MPG (l/100km) for ix20 range: Urban 34.0 (8.3) – 60.1 (4.7), Extra Urban 51.4 (5.5) – 67.3 (4.2), Combined 43.6 (6.5) – 65.7 (4.3), CO_2 154 – 114g/km.
5 Year Triple Care terms and exclusions apply. Please see www.hyundai.co.uk/owners/triple5 or ask your local dealer.

Page Ref	Provider	Street name	Type	Page Ref	Provider	Street name	Type
18 C4	Queens Park	Queens Park	WC	27 D4	Public Toilet	Tavistock Road	WC
18 C4	Queens Park	Queens Park, by Playground	↗	27 D4	Westbourne Grove	Colville Road	↗
19 D2	Tricycle Theatre & Cinema*	Kilburn High Road	↗	27 D4	Duke Of Wellington*	Portobello Road	↗
19 D2	Mecca Bingo*	Kilburn High Road	↗	27 D4	Public Toilet	Portobello Road	WC
19 D4	Public Toilet	Salusbury Road	WC	27 F1	Elgin Bar & Grill*	Elgin Avenue	↗
19 E3	Nandos *	Kilburn High Road	↗	27 F4	Public Toilet	Queensway	WC
19 E3	Caffe Nero *	102 Kilburn High Road	↗	27 F4	Public Toilet	Westbourne Grove	WC
19 E3	Public Toilet	Victoria Road/Kilburn High Street	↗	27 F4	Nandos*	63 Westbourne Grove	↗
20 C4	Wellington Place	by Lords Cricket Ground	↗	28 B1	Lords Cricket Ground*	St Johns Wood Road	↗
21 D3	Public Toilet	Albert Terrace	WC	28 B4	Paddington Station	Platform 1	↗
21 E4	Regents Park	Regents Park	WC	28 B4	Garfunkel's*	Praed Street	↗
21 F2	Ice Wharf*	Suffolk Wharf, Jamestown Road	↗	28 C4	Tyburn*	Edgware Road	↗
21 F2	Camden Lock Market *	Camden Lock	↗	28 C4	McDonald's*	178 Edgware Road	↗
21 F2	Jongleurs*	East Yard, Camden Lock	↗	28 C4	Grosvenor Victoria Casino*	Edgware Road	↗
21 F3	Public Toilet	Camden High Street	WC	29 D2	Marylebone Station	Concourse	↗
21 F3	The Crescent*	Camden High Street	↗	29 D3	Public Toilet	Marylebone Road	WC
21 F3	Edward's*	Camden High Street	↗	29 D3	Nandos*	113 Baker Street	↗
22 C4	Kings Cross Station	Platform 8	↗	29 D3	Globe*	Marylebone Road	↗
23 E1	London Met University*	Holloway Road	↗	29 D3	Metropolitan*	Station Approach, Marylebone Road	↗
23 E2	Albion*	Thornhill Road	↗	29 E1	Regents Park	Inner Circle	WC
23 E4	Steam Passage*	Upper Street	↗	29 E1	Regents Park	Chester Road	↗
23 E4	Chapel Market	White Conduit Street	↗	29 E2	Marylebone Road	opp Planetarium	↗
23 F2	The House*	Canonbury Road	↗	29 E3	Public Toilet	Marylebone Road	WC
23 F4	The Angel*	Islington High Street	↗	29 E3	Public Toilet	Paddington Street	WC
24 C4	Hoxton Market	Stanway Street	↗	29 E3	Public Toilet	Manchester Square	↗
24 F3	Islington Green	Essex Road	↗	29 E4	Public Toilet	Barrett Street	WC
25 E4	Public Toilet	Haggerston Park	WC	29 E4	Public Toilet	Oxford Street	WC
26 C3	Public Toilet	Bevington Road	WC	29 E4	Selfridges *	Oxford Street	↗
27 D2	Public Toilet	Walterton Road	WC	29 F1	Regents Park	Chester Road	WC
				29 F2	Public Toilet	Great Portland Street	WC
				29 F4	Plaza Centre*	Oxford Street	↗
				29 F4	John Lewis*	Oxford Street	↗

* Toilet is situated on private property

National Key Scheme toilet   WC Wheelchair accessible toilet   WC Public toilet

Page Ref	Provider	Street name	Type
30 A3	Nandos*	57/9 Goodge Street	NKS
30 A4	Public Toilet	Great Marlborough Street	WC
30 A4	O'Neill's*	Great Marlborough Street	NKS
30 B1	London Euston Station	Concourse	NKS
30 B4	All Bar One*	Cambridge Circus	NKS
30 B4	O'Neill's*	Wardour Street	NKS
30 B4	Public Toilet	Bedford Square	NKS
30 C2	Russell Square	opp Bernard Street	NKS
30 C2	Nandos*	The Brunswick Centre	NKS
30 C2	Marquis Cornwallis*	Russell Square	NKS
30 C4	All Bar One*	New Oxford Street	NKS
31 D2	Guilford Street	Guilford Street	WC
31 D3	High Holborn	opp Proctor Street	WC
31 D3	Pendrells Oak*	High Holborn	NKS
31 D3	High Holborn	opp Proctor Street	NKS
31 D4	All Bar One*	Kingsway	NKS
31 D4	Shakespeare's Head*	Kingsway	NKS
31 D4	Peacock Theatre*	Portugal Street	NKS
31 E2	Bar 38*	St Johns Street	NKS
31 E2	Sir John Oldcastle*	Farringdon Road	NKS
31 E2	Clerkenwell Road	Leather Lane	NKS
31 E2	Printworks*	Farringdon Road	NKS
31 E4	Knights Templar*	Chancery Lane	NKS
31 E4	Alibi*	Shoe Lane	NKS
31 E4	Hog's Head*	Fetter Lane	NKS
31 F3	Butchers Hook & Cleaver*	West Smithfield	NKS
31 F3	Three Compasses*	Cowcross Street	NKS
31 F4	St Bride Street	St Bride Street	WC
31 F4	Fleet Street	Fleet Street	WC
31 F4	All Bar One*	Ludgate Hill	NKS
31 F4	Leon*	Ludgate Circus	NKS
31 F4	New Change	St Pauls Churchyard	NKS
31 F4	Public Toilet	Paternoster Square	NKS
32 A1	Public Toilet	Macclesfield Road	WC
32 A1	Finsbury Leisure Centre*	Norman Street	NKS
32 A3	Public Toilet	Fore Street Avenue	WC
32 A3	Guildhall School of Music*	Silk Street	NKS
32 A4	Fine Line*	Bow Churchyard	NKS
32 A4	Public Toilet	Milk Street	WC
32 A4	Lord Raglan*	St Martin-Le-Grand	NKS
32 B3	All Bar One*	Finsbury Pavement	NKS
32 B3	Public Toilet	Moorgate, opp Market	NKS
32 B3	Caffè Nero*	London Wall	NKS
32 B3	Rack & Tenter*	Moorfields	NKS
32 B4	Green Man*	Poultry	NKS
32 C3	Public Toilet	Bishopsgate	WC
32 C3	Hamilton Hall*	Liverpool Street Station	NKS
32 C3	Liverpool Street Station	Platform 10	NKS
32 C3	Nandos*	Middlesex Street	NKS
32 C3	The Wren*	Liverpool Street Station	NKS
32 C4	Bishopsgate Institute*	Bishopsgate	NKS
32 C4	Slug & Lettuce*	St Mary Axe	NKS
32 C4	Crosse Keys*	Gracechurch Street	NKS
32 C4	Slug & Lettuce*	St Mary Axe	NKS
32 F4	The Paternoster*	Paternoster Square	NKS
33 C4	Public Toilet	Harrow Place	WC
33 C4	All Bar One*	Houndsditch	NKS
33 C4	Slug & Lettuce*	Stoney Lane	NKS
33 D1	Public Toilet	Columbia Road	WC
33 D2	Nandos	114 Commercial Street	NKS
33 D2	Whitechapel Market	Commercial Road	NKS
33 D2	Nandos*	366 Bethnal Green Road	NKS

Page Ref	Provider	Street name	Type
33 D3	Public Toilet	Leyden Street	WC
33 D4	Public Toilet	Aldgate	WC
33 D4	Bar 38*	Derbyshire Street	↗
33 D4	Bar 38*	St Clare House, Minories	↗
33 E1	Public Toilet	Derbyshire Street	WC
33 E4	Public Toilet	Whitechapel Road	WC
34 A3	Vue Cinema*	Shepherds Bush Green	↗
34 A3	Walkabout*	Shepherds Bush Green	↗
34 B3	Central Bar*	West 12 Shopping Centre	↗
34 B4	Blythe Road	Blythe Road	WC
34 C4	Kensington*	Russell Gardens	↗
35 D3	Public Toilet	Phillimore Walk	WC
35 D3	Kensington Memorial Park	St Marks Road	↗
35 D4	Holland Park	Ilchester Place	↗
35 D4	Napier Road	Napier Road	↗
35 E2	Nandos*	58 Notting Hill Gate	↗
35 E3	Public Toilet	Kensington High Street, by Cinema	↗
35 E3	Kensington Town Hall	Town Hall Car Park	↗
35 F1	Public Toilet	Bayswater Road	WC
36 A1	Public Toilet	Lancaster Gate	WC
36 A3	Kensington Road	Kensington Road, opp Palace Gate	↗
36 A4	Black Widow*	Gloucester Road	↗
37 D1	Public Toilet	Marble Arch	WC
37 E1	Balderton Street	Off Oxford Street	↗
37 F2	Public Toilet	Stratton Street	WC
37 F2	Public Toilet & Changing Places	The Queens Walk	WC
38 A2	Green Park	Next to Station	WC
38 A3	St James's Park	Marlborough Gate	↗
38 A4	Bressenden Place	Bressenden Place/ Victoria Street	↗
38 A4	Nandos*	17 Cardinal Walk	↗
38 B1	Moon Under Water*	Leicester Square	↗
38 B1	Chiquito*	Leicester Square	↗
38 B1	O'Neill's*	Wardour Street	↗
38 B1	Piccadilly Circus Station Subway	Steps on approach	↗
38 B1	Yates*	Leicester Square	↗
38 B1	Brewmaster*	Cranbourne Street	↗
38 B1	Odeon*	Leicester Square	↗
38 B1	Montagu Pyke*	Charing Cross Road	↗
38 B2	St James's Park	St James's Park	WC
38 B3	Broad Sanctuary	Broad Sanctuary	↗
38 B3	Cabinet War Rooms*	King Charles Street	↗
38 C1	Nandos*	66-8 Chandos Place	↗
38 C1	Ha! Ha! Bar*	Villiers Street	↗
38 C1	Walkabout*	Henrietta Street	↗
38 C2	Public Toilet & Changing Places	Victoria Embankment Gardens	WC
38 C2	Lord Moon Of The Mall*	Whitehall	↗
38 C2	Victoria Embankment Garden	by Underground Station	↗
38 C2	Charing Cross Station	Charing Cross	↗
39 A2	Green Park	Green Park	WC
39 C1	Strand	Strand/Arundel Street	↗
39 D1	Columbia Bar*	Aldwych	↗
39 D1	Walkabout*	Temple Place	↗
39 E2	Gabriels Wharf*	Gabriels Wharf	↗
39 E3	Waterloo East Station	Platform B/C	↗
39 E3	Waterloo Station	Concourse & Forecourt	↗
39 F1	Blackfriars Station*	Concourse	↗
39 F2	Founders Arms*	Hopton Street	↗
40 A1	Public Toilet & Changing Places	Bankside	WC
40 A2	Tate Modern*	Tate Modern	↗

* Toilet is situated on private property

Page Ref	Provider	Street name	Type	Page Ref	Provider	Street name	Type
40 B1	Public Toilet	Eastcheap	WC	43 E4	Nandos*	20 Fulham Broadway	NKS
40 B1	Fine Line*	Monument Street	NKS	43 E4	Oyster Rooms*	Fulham Broadway	NKS
40 B1	The Banker*	Cousin Lane	NKS	43 E4	Vanston Place	Fulham Broadway	NKS
40 B1	Cannon Street Station	Lower Concourse	NKS	44 A1	Public Toilet	Gloucester Road	WC
40 B2	Public Toilet	London Bridge Street	WC	44 A1	Nandos*	117 Gloucester Road	NKS
40 B2	London Bridge Station	Platform 5/6	NKS	44 B1	South Kensington Station	South Kensington Station	WC
40 B2	London Bridge Station	Forecourt	NKS	45 D4	Prince Albert*	Albert Bridge Road	NKS
40 B2	Market Porter*	Stoney Street	NKS	45 E1	Victoria Coach Station	Departure Hall	NKS
40 B2	All Bar One*	London Bridge Street	NKS	45 E1	Travellers Tavern*	Elizabeth Street	NKS
40 D2	Nandos*	225 Clink Street	NKS	45 E4	Battersea Park	Battersea Park	WC
40 B3	Public Toilet	Borough High Street	WC	45 F1	Shakespeare*	Buckingham Palace Road	NKS
40 C1	Caffè Nero*	London Street	NKS	45 F1	Victoria Place Shopping Centre	Buckingham Palace Road	NKS
40 C1	Public Toilet	Great Tower Street	WC				
40 C1	Public Toilet	Lovat Lane	WC	45 F1	Victoria Station	Concourse	NKS
40 C1	Public Toilet	Tower Hill	WC	46 A1	Tachbrook Street	by market	NKS
40 C1	Fenchurch Street Station	Lower Level	NKS	46 A1	Willow Walk*	Wilton Road	NKS
40 C1	Liberty Bounds*	Trinity Square	NKS	46 A1	Nandos*	107 Wilton Road	NKS
40 C2	GLA*	City Hall	NKS	46 B1	Public Toilet	Horseferry Road	WC
41 C4	Pommelers Rest*	Tower Bridge Road	NKS	46 C3	Bondway Bus Station	Bondway	WC
41 D1	Goodman's Fields*	Mansell Street	NKS	46 C3	Vauxhall Bus Station	Thorporch Road	WC
41 D2	All Bar One*	Butlers Wharf	NKS	48 A1	Public Toilet	Elephant & Castle	WC
41 F4	Public Toilet & Changing Places	Keetons Road	WC	48 A1	Public Toilet	Walworth Road	WC
42 A2	Hammersmith Broadway Centre	Hammersmith Bridge	NKS	48 A3	Gala Bingo*	Camberwell Road	NKS
				48 B2	Public Toilet	Dawes Street	WC
42 A2	Kings Mall Shopping Centre	Kings Street	NKS	48 B2	Public Toilet	Portland Street	WC
				48 B3	Public Toilet	Wells Way	WC
42 A2	Hammersmith Apollo*	Hammersmith Apollo	NKS	49 E3	Asda*	Old Kent Road	WC
42 A3	Crabtree*	Rainville Road	NKS	51 D1	Asda*	Marshall Street	WC
42 B3	Public Toilet	Lillie Road	WC	52 A3	Public Toilet	Roman Road	WC
43 D3	Public Toilet	North End Road	WC	53 F1	West Ham Lane	Recreational Ground	WC
43 E1	Earls Court Station	Earls Court	WC				
43 E1	McDonald's*	208 Earls Court Road	NKS				
43 E4	Public Toilet	Effie Place	WC				

Host Airport

Heathrow
Making every journey better.

London Airports

General Information Travelling from Airports

For security reasons the Blue Badge scheme does not operate at most airports. However airports are required to provide assistance to disabled and reduced mobility passengers at the airport between their aircraft seat and the airport arrival or departure point. Additional help phones are installed as part of the measures to offer assistance. These are typically sited adjacent to Blue Badge bays and car park entrances as well as around the terminal.

Luton Airport

Free assistance is available to disabled customers via the special assistance telephones sited in car parks and around the terminal building. This service includes assistance to the check-in desk or from the arrivals area to the short term car park, terminal bus stops or taxi rank.

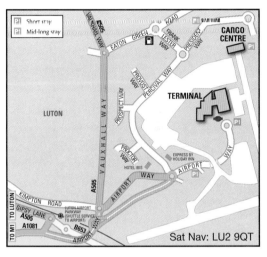

Sat Nav: LU2 9QT

There are designated disabled parking bays and help points in all the car parks with the mid term and long term car parks serviced by an accessible shuttle bus. In the short term car park Blue Badge holders can park in the designated bays for the first 60 minutes free of charge. Blue badge holders need to leave their parking clock on display in the vehicle whilst validating their concession at the NCP payment desk in arrivals. Pre-booking discount is available if you book online.

Passengers can also be dropped off in the Drop Off Zone. There is a charge, however vehicles cannot be left unattended.

General enquiries call **01582 405100** or email **disabledfacilities@ltn.aero**
For car park enquiries and travelling with a motorised wheelchair contact:
APCOA on **0845 303 7397** or **07809 492373** (21.00 to 09.00).

London City Airport

There are designated disabled parking bays and a help point situated within the short stay car park close to the terminal. They have dedicated staff to assist passengers with reduced mobility from the short stay car park and Drop Off Zone to the terminal.

Contact Customer Services on **0207 646 0000** or
cscsupervisor@londoncityairport.com for further information.   Sat Nav: E16 2PX

Heathrow general information: **www.heathrowairport.com**
For more information on travelling through Heathrow with reduced mobility call **0208 757 2700**

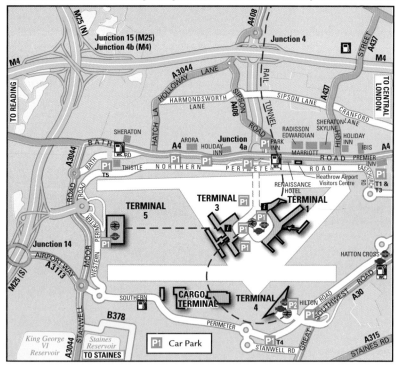

Sat Nav:
Terminal 1: TW6 1AP, Terminal 3: TW6 1QG, Terminal 4: TW6 3XA, Terminal 5: TW6 2GA

Help points

Free assistance is available for those with special needs. Help points are located on terminal forecourts, short-stay car parks, in stations and in baggage reclaim halls. There is also a free wheelchair-accessible service to assist passengers with reduced mobility.

If you arrive at the coach station and need assistance to terminals 1, 2 or 3 then use the help point located en route to the underground.

Inform your airline of your particular need **at the time of booking** or at least **48 hours** before your travel. Please look for the special assistance host desks, before security in all of the terminals. Alternately use the help points for assistance

Help bus (between all terminals)

To call a help bus use the green help point or special bus telephones in arrivals or at stand 6 at the central bus station. Buses are limited and it is advisable to allow additional time for your journey.

Gatwick Airport

Gatwick general information: telephone **0844 892 0322** and select option 2

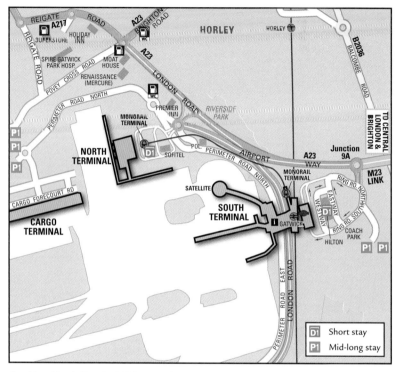

Sat Nav: North Terminal RH6 0NP, South Terminal RH6 0PJ

Help points

Designated Blue Badge bays are available in the multi-storey short stay car parks of both terminals with accessible routes into the terminals. Special assistance help points are located near the reserved parking spaces and assistance is free to those with special needs. Priority for assistance is likely to be given to those who have pre-booked with their airline or travel agent.

If you wish to park in a designated bay but take your badge abroad, you will need to show your badge to the car park operator. Please contact the car park operator via the help button on the car park entry machine.

YOUR LONDON AIRPORT
Gatwick

Stansted Airport

Stansted general information: **www.stanstedairport.com**

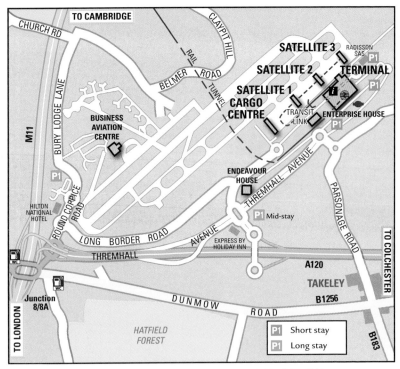

For more information call the BAA information line on **0844 335 1000**
Sat Nav: CM24 1RW. Email: info.prm@uk.issworld.com

Help points

Help Phones are located beside each of the main terminal entry doors. There are also Help Call Points along the outer lane pavement of the set-down zone on the terminal forecourt, as well as in each zone of the Short-stay car park.

If arriving by coach yellow help points are situated on the pavement between the coach station and the terminal.

The helpdesk for passengers requiring special assistance is located at the front of the terminal building, between check-in zones D & E and is staffed 24 hours a day.

Blue Badge parking is available in short term car parks Red, Orange, Green, Fast Track and Pick Up car parks which are located next to the terminal building.

The mid stay car park is situated approx 1 mile and the long stay is approx 4 miles from the terminal building. All transfer coaches are wheelchair accessible.

Blue Badge parking spaces are situated close to the bus shelter & help point in the Mid-stay car park zone L and Long-stay zone Q.

London
Stansted ↗
Go discover

Explore the Capital with myaccesslondon.com

Name	Address	Page/Ref	Contact	Car Park
Barnes Hospital (NHS)	South Worple Way, Barnes, SW14 8SU	outside map area	020 8878 8151	Y
Central Middlesex Hospital (NHS)	Acton Lane, Park Royal, NW10 7NS	outside map area	020 8965 5733	Y
Charing Cross Hospital (NHS)	Fulham Palace Road, Hammersmith, W6 8RF	42 B3	020 8846 1234	Y
Chelsea & Westminster Hospital (NHS)	369 Fulham Road, Kensington & Chelsea, SW10 9NH	44 A3	020 8746 8000	Y
Cromwell Hospital (Private)	Cromwell Road, South Kensington, SW5 0TU	43 F1	020 7460 2000	N
Edgware Community Hospital (NHS)	Burnt Oak Broadway, Edgware, HA8 0AD	outside map area	020 8952 2381	Y
Finchley Memorial Hospital (NHS)	Granville Road, North Finchley, N12 0JE	outside map area	020 8349 7500	Y
Gordon Hospital (NHS)	Bloomberg Street, Pimlico, SW1V 2RH	46 B1	020 8746 8733	N
Great Ormond Street Children's Hospital (NHS)	34 Great Ormond Street, Russell Square, WC1N 3JH	31 D2	0207 405 9200	N
Guy's Hospital (NHS)	Great Maze Pond, London Bridge, SE1 9RT	40 B3	020 7188 7188	Y
Hammersmith or Queen Charlotte's Hospital (NHS)	Du Cane Road, East Acton, W12 0HS	outside map area	020 8383 1111	Y
Harley Street Clinic (Private)	35 Weymouth Street, Marylebone, W1G 8BJ	29 F3	020 7935 7700	N
Homerton University Hospital (NHS)	Homerton Row, Homerton, E9 6SR	outside map area	020 8510 5555	Y
Hospital For Tropical Diseases (NHS)	Mortimer Market Centre, Mortimer Market, Off Capper Street, Bloomsbury, WC1E 6JD	30 A2	020 3456 7890	N
Hospital Of St John & St Elizabeth (Private)	60 Grove End Road, St John's Wood, NW8 9NH	28 B1	020 7806 4000	N
Kings College Hospital (NHS)	Bessemer Road, Denmark Hill, SE5 9RS	outside map area	020 3299 9000	Y
Lambeth Hospital (NHS)	108 Landor Road, Lambeth, SW9 9NX	outside map area	020 3228 6000	Y
London Bridge Hospital (Private)	27 Tooley Street, London Bridge, SE1 2PR	40 C2	020 7407 3100	Y
Marie Curie Hospice (Private)	11 Lyndhurst Gardens, Hampstead, NW3 5NS	outside map area	020 7853 3400	Y
Mile End Hospital (NHS)	275 Bancroft Road, Mile End, E1 4DG	outside map area	020 7377 7000	N
Moorfields Eye Hospital (NHS)	162 City Road, St Luke's, EC1V 2PD	32 B1	020 7253 3411	N
National Hospital For Neurology and Neurosciences (NHS)	Queen Square, Bloomsbury, WC1N 3BG	30 C2	020 7837 3611	N
Newham General Hospital (NHS)	Glen Road, Plaistow, E13 8SL	outside map area	020 7476 4000	Y
Northwick Park & St Mark's (NHS)	Watford Road, Harrow, HA1 3UJ	outside map area	020 8864 3232	Y
Parkside Hospital (Private)	53 Parkside, Wimbledon, SW19 5NX	outside map area	020 8971 8000	Y
Portland Hospital For Women & Children (Private)	205-209 Great Portland Street, Bloomsbury, W1W 5AH	29 F3	020 7580 4400	N
Portman Clinic (NHS)	8 Fitzjohn's Avenue, Hampstead, NW3 5NA	outside map area	020 7794 8262	N
Princess Grace Hospital (Private)	42-52 Nottingham Place, Marylebone, W1U 5NY	29 E2	020 7486 1234	N
Queen Elizabeth Hospital (NHS)	Stadium Road, Woolwich, SE18 4QH	outside map area	020 8836 6000	Y
Queen Mary's Hospital (NHS)	Roehampton Lane, Roehampton, SW15 5PN	outside map area	020 8487 6000	Y
Royal Brompton Hospital (NHS)	Sydney Street, South Kensington, SW3 6NP	44 C2	020 7352 8121	Y

General Car Park Information	Blue Badge Parking
Free car park located in hospital grounds.	3 Blue Badge parking bays available. Collect a permit from reception.
On-site car parking is available.	Limited number of Blue Badge bays are free to permit holders.
On-site car parking is available.	Parking is free for Blue Badge holders in any of the available spaces.
Underground car park with limited spaces.	Parking is free for Blue Badge holders in any of the available spaces. Must Display Blue Badge and time clock.
Short term parking is available in the immediate vicinity on parking meters. Long stay parking available at the Marriott Hotel car park.	No Disabled parking available.
Limited Pay & Display parking bays in hospital car park.	A number of Blue Badge bays are available. If full then any bay can be used for free when displaying your Blue Badge and time clock.
A limited number of visitor parking spaces.	A number of Blue Badge bays are available.
On-site car parking is not available,	No Disabled parking available.
On-street Pay & Display. On-site car parking is not available.	On-street Blue Badge parking spaces are available in the immediate area of the hospital.
Limited parking available.	There is limited disabled parking in the car park and a drop off facility.
Public car park to the rear of hospitals.	Free Blue Badge parking in any of the available spaces.
2 Blue Badge bays for appointment holders.	Other Blue Badge bays available in Weymouth St. & Harley St.
On-street Pay & Display.	Blue Badge bays adjacent to the main entrance to the hospital.
On-site car parking is not available.	Pay & Display bays in the local area.
Public Car Park in Kingsmill Terrace.	Pay & Display bays in the local area.
Parking opposite the main entrance at Hambleden Wing and Golden Jubilee Wing entrance.	Blue Badge bays are located outside Bessemer Rd entrance and outside A&E. 3 disabled bays are available off site in Venetian Rd. There are no exemptions in general car park.
Limited parking at the Lambeth Hospital. Parking is difficult in some of the nearby streets.	Blue Badge parking is available at hospital entrance.
The nearest car park is Snowfields NCP on Kipling Street.	2 Blue Badge Badge bays at hospital entrance, call in advance to book.
Limited parking in the hospice grounds.	Blue badge holders may park in designated bays free of charge.
On-street Pay & Display.	There are 12 parking spaces for disabled badge holders on-site and outside the therapy centre in Longnor Rd.
On-street Pay & Display bays are limited. Nearest car park is 10 minutes walk away along City Road at Finsbury Square.	Off street Pay & Display.
Limited on-street Pay & Display. Nearest NCP Southampton Row.	On-street Blue Badge parking and Pay & Display.
Limited car parking is available in the hospital grounds.	A limited number of Blue Badge bays exist in the hospital car park
Parking is available throughout the hospital grounds in car parks 1 (multi-storey), 2, 3 and 4; these locations are signposted from the hospital ring road.	Parking is free for disabled people or their carers when driving a disabled person to hospital. Vehicles must park in designated bays and show a valid Blue Badge.
On-site car parking is available.	Disabled parking is available on site.
Visitors have the option of two car parks close by to the hospital; the NCP in Carburton Street or Pure Parking in Devonshire Row Mews.	No on-site disabled bays (Nearest bay opposite the hospital).
On-street Pay & Display.	2 Blue Badge bays. If full park in another space with Blue Badge permit. For patients and visitors only to the Taverstock & Portman clinics.
On-street Pay & Display.	Blue Badge bay on-site, for the use of patients or visitors only.
Total of 356 car park spaces.	Blue Badge holders may park in any of the designated bays free of charge.
On-site parking available.	Blue Badge holders may park in any of the designated bays.
Hospital parking is three minutes' walk away in the Sydney Street NCP or on-street parking.	Limited spaces available in front of Sydney Wing for Blue Badge holders.

Name	Address	Page/Ref	Contact	Car Park
Royal Free Hospital (NHS)	10 Pond Street, Hampstead, NW3 2QG	**outside map area**	020 7794 0500	Y
Royal London Homeopathic Hospital (NHS)	60 Great Ormond Street, Queens Square, WC1N 3HR	**31** D2	020 3448 2000	N
Royal Marsden Hospital (NHS)	197 Fulham Road, South Kensington, SW3 6NP	**44** C1	020 7352 8171	N
Royal National Orthopaedic Hospital (NHS) (out patients only)	45-51 Bolsover Street, Marylebone, W1W 5AQ	**29** F2	020 8954 2300	Y
St Bartholomew's Hospital (NHS)	West Smithfield, St Pauls, EC1A 7BE	**31** F3	020 7377 7000	N
St George's Hospital (NHS)	Blackshaw Road, Tooting, SW17 0QT	**outside map area**	020 8672 1255	Y
St Mary's Hospital (NHS)	Praed Street, Paddington, W2 1NY	**28** B4	020 7886 6666	N
St Pancras Hospital (NHS)	4 St Pancras Way, St Pancras, NW1 0PE	**22** B3	020 3317 3500	N
St Thomas' Hospital (NHS)	Westminster Bridge Road, Westminster, SE1 7EH	**39** D3	020 7188 7188	Y
St Charles Hospital (NHS)	Exmoor Street, North Kensington, W10 6DZ	**26** B3	020 8206 7000	N
The Eastman Dental Hospital (NHS)	256 Gray's Inn Road, St Pancras, WC1X 8LD	**31** D2	020 7915 1000	N
The Heart Hospital (NHS)	16-18 Westmoreland Street, Marylebone, W1G 8PH	**29** E3	020 3456 7898	N
The Huntercombe Roehampton Hospital (Private)	Holybourne Avenue, Roehampton, SW15 4JL	**outside map area**	020 8780 6155	Y
The Lister Hospital (Private)	Chelsea Bridge Road, Pimlico, SW1W 8RH	**45** F2	020 7881 4000	Y
The London Chest Hospital (NHS)	Bonner Road, Bethnal Green, E2 9JX	**outside map area**	020 7377 7000	N
The London Clinic (Private)	20 Devonshire Place, Marylebone, W1G 6BW	**29** F3	020 7935 4444	N
The Royal London Hospital (NHS)	Whitechapel Road, Whitechapel, E1 1BB	**33** F3	020 7377 7000	N
The Royal National Throat, Nose & Ear Hospital (NHS)	330 Gray's Inn Road, King's Cross, WC1X 8DA	**31** D1	020 7915 1300	N
The Whittington Hospital (NHS)	Magdala Avenue, Archway, N19 5NF	**outside map area**	020 7272 3070	Y
University College Hospital (NHS)	235 Euston Road, Euston, NW1 2BU	**30** A2	020 3456 7890	N
University Hospital Lewisham (NHS)	Lewisham High Street, Lewisham, SE13 6LH	**outside map area**	020 8333 3000	Y
Wanstead Hospital (NHS)	Makepeace Road, Wanstead, E11 1UU	**outside map area**	020 8539 5522	N
Wellington Hospital (Private)	8A Wellington Place, St John's Wood, NW8 9LE	**20** C2	020 7483 5148	N
Western Eye Hospital (Private)	153-173 Marylebone Road, Paddington, NW1 5QH	**28** C3	020 7886 6666	N
Whipps Cross University Hospital (NHS)	Whipps Cross Road, Whipps Cross, E11 1NR	**outside map area**	020 8539 5522	Y
Willesden Hospital (NHS)	Harlesden Road, Willesden, NW10 3RY	**outside map area**	020 8438 7000	Y

General Car Park Information	Blue Badge Parking
On-street Pay & Display.	Disabled badge holders may park in any of the designated Blue Badge bays outside A&E and the main entrance but must display badge.
On-street Pay & Display.	5 parking spaces in Dudmaston Mews can be reserved in advance by calling 020 7351 8012.
On-street Pay & Display. The nearest car park is located at Sydney Street.	Few metered bays and some disabled bays in Dudmaston Mews.
Parking available at the Holiday Inn NCP, Carburton Street.	3 Blue Badge bays are available outside Bolsover St entrance. Pay & Display and Pay by Phone bays where Blue Badge holders can stay for 1 extra hour for free after making an initial payment for parking.
Limited on-street Pay & Display bays. The nearest car park is the NCP on West Smithfield Street.	Nearest on-street Blue badge bays are located on Giltspur Street, West Smithfield and Bartholmew Close.
Pay on exit car park access on Blackshaw Road and Fountain Road.	Blue Badge holders may park free in the reserved disabled bays near the entrances and in white painted bays on the hospital perimeter road.
Off street Pay & Display.	On-street Blue Badge bays within 200 metres of the hospital on S Wharf Road and Winsland Street.
Off street Pay & Display.	On Site disabled Blue Badge bays available. Check if visitors parking is available call 020 3317 3554.
Parking for patients and visitors is very limited. Alternative parking is available in on-street Pay & Display bays.	Parking is free for disabled patients displaying a Blue Badge clock with an appointment. Take permit and appointment card to the security desk.
Limited hospital Pay & Display bays.	3 disabled bays on site. If full, you may park in other bays and inform reception if you take up a non Blue Badge bay.
On-street metered and Pay & Display parking is limited to a two hour stay. Public car parking (National Car Parks) is nearby in Brunswick Square.	Limited Blue Badge parking bays are located in the Victoria Wing Yard, accessible via the archway entrance at 256 Gray's Inn Road.
Limited on-street parking.	Parking is on-street Pay & Display bays, payment required between 8.30 and 18.30.
On-site car parking is available.	1 Blue Badge bay on site. If bay is full, Blue Badge holders can park in another bay as long as a patient or visitor to the hospital.
On-site car parking is available for patients.	Disabled bay on-street outside. In car park space for patients only. Book at least 24 hours in advance.
On-street Pay & Display.	Pay & Display Valance Road.
On-street Pay & Display.	Nearest Blue Badge bay is opposite the hospital's main entrance.
On-street Pay & Display bays available. Nearest car park is located in New Road.	Blue badge holders can park on the single yellow lines outside the hospital for a maximum of 3 hours -must display blue badge. Car park in Sydney St. has Blue Badge bays & is free.
On-street Pay & Display bays available. Nearest car park is located in Britannia street.	Swinton Street car park has dedicated Blue Badge bays.
Parking is allowed between 6pm and 8am Mondays to Fridays and all day at the weekends.	8 Blue Badge bays available free to use before 6pm. Pay & Display from 6pm to 8am.
General disabled parking on the Camden side of Euston Road.	Disabled parking available for outpatients. Dispensation available at the hospital on receipt of appointment letter and Blue Badge.
Limited Pay & Display parking on-site for patients and visitors.	Disabled drivers may park free for their first 4 hours providing they are parked in a marked disabled bay.
Off street Pay & Display.	Blue Badge bays are situated outside Heronewood Galion Unit.
On-street Pay & Display parking available. Nearest Car Park at Kingsmill Terrace. On cricket free days, Lord's also offers parking facilities.	No on-site disabled bays. Nearest Blue Badge bay opposite the hospital's main entrance.
Off street Pay & Display.	Blue Badge bays situated on-site.
Several Pay & Display car parks at the hospital.	Blue Badge parking bays on-site for Blue Badge holders.
On-site Pay & Display.	Blue Badge parking bays on-site for Blue Badge holders.

Name	Address	Page/Ref	Contact	Website
Athletics				
Crystal Palace National Sports Centre	Ledrington Road, SE19 2BB	**Outside map area**	020 8778 0131	www.gll.org/centre/crystal-palace national-sports-centre.asp
Cricket				
Lord's Cricket Ground	St John's Wood, NW8 8QN	**28** B1	020 7616 8500	www.lords.org
The Oval	Surrey County Cricket Club, Kennington, SE11 5SS	**47** D3	020 7820 5700	www.kiaoval.com
Football				
Arsenal F.C.	Emirates Stadium, Drayton Park, N5 1BU	**Outside map area**	020 7619 5003	www.arsenal.com
Barnet F.C.	Underhill Stadium, Barnet Lane, EN5 2DN	**Outside map area**	020 8441 6932	www.barnetfc.com
Chelsea F.C.	Chelsea Football Club, Stamford Bridge, Fulham Road, SW6 1HS	**43** F4	020 7915 2200	www.chelseafc.com
Crystal Palace F.C.	Selhurst Park, SE25 6PU	**Outside map area**	020 8768 6000	www.cpfc.co.uk
Fulham F.C.	Craven Cottage, Stevenage Road, SW6 6HH	**Outside map area**	0870 442 1222	www.fulhamfc.com
Millwall F.C.	Zampa Road, SE16 3LN	**Outside map area**	020 7232 1222	www.millwallfc.premiumtv.co.uk
Queens Park Rangers	South Africa Road, W12 7PJ	**Outside map area**	020 8743 0262	www.qpr.premiumtv.co.uk
Tottenham Hotspur	Bill Nicholson Way, 748 High Road, Tottenham, N17 OAP	**Outside map area**	020 8365 5161	www.tottenhamhotspur.com
Wembley Stadium	South Way, Wembley, HA9 0WS	**Outside map area**	0844 980 8001	www.wembleystadium.com
West Ham United	Boleyn Ground, Green Street, Upton Park, E13 9AZ	**Outside map area**	0845 217 1332	www.whufc.com
Greyhound Racing				
GRA Wimbledon Stadium	Plough Lane, SW17 0BL	**Outside map area**	0870 840 8905	www.lovethedogs.co.uk
Rugby				
Twickenham Stadium Rugby Football Union	Rugby House, Rugby Road, Twickenham, TW1 1DZ	**Outside map area**	0871 222 2017	www.rfu.com
Tennis				
The All England Lawn Tennis Club	Church Road, Wimbledon, SW19 5AE	**Outside map area**	0208 944 1066	www.wimbledon.com
The Queen's Club	Palliser Road, West Kensington, W14 9EQ	**42** C2	020 7385 3421	www.queensclub.co.uk
Miscellaneous				
The O2 Arena	The O2 Peninsula Square, West Parkside, SE10 0DX	**Outside map area**	020 8463 3359	www.theo2.co.uk
Olympia	Hammersmith Road, W14 8UX	**34** C4	020 7385 1200	www.eco.co.uk
Wembley Arena	Wembley Stadium Complex, Empire Way, HA9 0DW	**Outside map area**	020 8782 5500	www.wembleyarena.co.uk

Venue car park	Blue Badge bay parking	Alternative parking
Yes on site	Yes	Street parking
Yes	No dedicated bays - limited parking must be reserved in advance. Call 020 7616 0050	Lanark Road Car Park, Bell St Master Park
No	Parking for Blue Badge holders is available on or near the site (depending on fixture) Call 020 7820 5678	Car Park on Vauxhall Bridge Rd
Yes on site	100 Blue Badge bays, Prebook 020 7704 4492 or 07806 285645	National Car Park, Sobell Centre, Highbury
Yes on site	3 Blue Badge bays for home supporters	High Barnet Underground Station Car Park
Yes on site	Limited on site parking Tel 0871 984 1955	Broadwood Terrace NCP
No	On street parking	Sainsbury's Car Park (Free after 13.30 Sat)
No	Parking bays allocated on a first come first served basis. Contact Disability Officer on 020 8336 7420	Henley Compton School booked 7 days in advance
Yes on site	10 Blue Badge bays for home supporters and 1 for away supporters. Contact Disabled Liaison Officer 020 7740 0512	Street parking around Deptford Park
No	Limited parking contact Disability Liaison Officer 020 8740 2545	BBC car park (match days only) in Wood Lane
Yes on site	Limited parking in West Stand and Paxton Road. Allocated on a first come first served basis. Blue Badge holders can park for max 5 hours in residents bays on match days	St Francis De Sales School (directly opposite Bill Nicholson Way) or on street parking bays
Yes (pre-book)	Yes - Limited number of pre-bookable spaces available. Apply via www.csparking.com/stadium	On street parking
Yes on site	Pre-allocated to season ticket holders. Street parking other option	On street parking or Newham General Hospital
Yes on site	Yes	On street parking
Yes (pre-book)	Yes (Apply via carparking@theRFU.com)	NCP Drummond Place
Yes on site	Yes (Car Parks 8 & 10)	Car parks located on Hatfield Crescent and St Georges Road
Yes on site	On street Blue Badge bays and resident bays	Olympia Way car park or Earls Court Seagraves Road car park
Yes on site	Blue Badge bays situated by entrances and exits. Prebook tel 020 8463 3359	North Greenwich London Underground NCP There is also a dedicated accessible drop off and pick up point for cars and coaches
Yes on site	Disabled bays require pre-booking Tel 020 7598 2515	Olympia Motorail Car Park Olympia MSCP Access on Maclise Road
Yes on site	Blue Badge concessionary car park passes available. Book online at www.csparking.com	Brook Ave car park, Wembley Park underground station

THE PIE GUIDE BLUE BADGE DOWNLOADS FOR SAT NAV USERS

TomTom and **Garmin** sat nav users can download Blue Badge data to your device, creating a journey planner custom-made for disabled drivers and their carers.

Features include:

➡ **Blue Badge parking bays across the UK**

➡ **Disabled accessible car parks**

➡ **Petrol stations (with Service Call)**

➡ **Tolls with concessions**

Head to The Pie Guide's website and download the Blue Badge data package in less than 5 minutes!

How to purchase
TomTom and Garmin downloads are available now for £29.99

Visit **www.thepieguide.com/shop** and click on the Blue Badge products for more information and how to order. Alternatively, call The Pie Guide on **0844 847 0875**.

Increasingly drivers are relying on satellite navigation to get to their desired location. To help you find your way we have included a list of useful postcodes to places of interest in London to make your journey easier.

10 Downing Street	SW1A 2AB	Lindsey House	SW10 0DG	Royal Fusiliers Museum	EC3N 4EE
Admiralty Arch	WC2N 5DW	Lloyds	EC3M 7BS	Royal Hospital Chelsea	SW3 4SR
Albert Memorial	SW7 1QH	London Aquarium	SE1 7JA	Royal London Hospital Museum	E1 1BZ
All Souls Church	W1B 1JA	London Canal Museum	N1 9RR	Royal Mews	SW1E 6HE
Apsley House	W1J 7NT	London Dungeon	SE1 2QF	Science Museum	SW7 3WZ
Baden Powell House	SW7 5JS	London Eye	SE1 7ND	Severs Dennis House	E1 6BX
Bank of England Museum	EC2R 8AH	London Fire Brigade Museum	SE1 0ER	Shakespeare Globe Museum	SE1 9DR
Banqueting House	SW1A 2ET	London Toy and Model Museum	W2 3ER	Sir John Soanes Museum	WC2A 3ED
Barbican Centre	EC1A 4JA	London Transport Museum	WC2E 8AA	Sothebys	W1S 2RS
Bethnal Green Museum of Childhood	E2 9LQ	London Zoo	NW1 4RY	South Bank Centre	SE1 8XU
British Museum	WC1B 3BE	Lord's Cricket Ground	NW8 6AA	South London Gallery	SE5 7DD
Buckingham Palace	SW1A 1AA	Madame Tussauds	NW1 5LR	Southwark Cathedral	SE1 9AG
Business Design Centre	N1 0PB	Mansion House	EC4N 8BH	Space Studios	SE11 5RP
Butlers Wharf	SE1 2LZ	MCC Museum	NW8 8QN	Spencer House	SW1A 1NR
Cabinet War Rooms	SW1A 2AH	Michael Faradays Museum	W1S 4BS	St Brides Church	EC4Y 8AU
Camden Market	NW1 8AB	Monument	EC3R 8AH	St Clement Danes	WC2R 1EF
Cenotaph	SW1A 2NH	Museum of Garden History	SE1 7JT	St Dunstan-in-the-East	EC3R 8DX
Clarence House	SW1A 1BA	Museum of London	EC2Y 5HN	St Giles Cripplegate	EC2Y 8DU
Covent Garden Market	WC2E 8PP	Museum of Mankind	W1S 3EP	St Helens Bishopsgate	EC3A 6HX
Design Museum	SE1 2YA	Museum of The Order of Saint John	EC1M 4DN	St James's Church	W1J 9EY
Dickens House Museum and Library	WC1N 2LW	National Army Museum	SW3 4EX	St James's Palace	SW1A 1BS
Earls Court	SW5 9TB	National Gallery	SW1Y 5BJ	St Martin in the Fields	WC2N 4JJ
Excel	E16 1XL	National Portrait Gallery	WC2N 5DN	St Pauls Cathedral	EC4M 8AD
Florence Nightingale Museum	SE1 7ER	Natural History Museum	SW9 7RT	St Pauls Church	WC2E 8SG
Foundation of Women's Art	EC1V 0AL	Nelsons Column	WC2N 5DP	Tate Britain	SW1P 4RG
Goldsmiths Hall	EC2V 6BN	New Spitalfields Market	E10 5SQ	Tate Modern	SE1 9JN
Guards Museum	SW1E 6HQ	Old Operating Theatre	SE1 9RG	Temple Church	EC4Y 1BW
Guildhall	EC2V 5AA	Olympia	W14 8UX	The Mall	SW1A 2BN
Hackney Museum	E8 1GR	Olympic Park	E20 2ST	Theatre Museum	WC2 7PR
Harrods	SW3 1EX	Palace of Westminster	SW1A 2JX	Tower Bridge Museum & Exhibition	E1W 1LD
Hayward Gallery	SE1 8AB	Parliament Square	SW1P 3JX	Tower of London	EC3N 1JY
History of Medicine Gallery	WC1H 0BE	Piccadilly Circus	W1J 9HW	Trafalgar Square	SW1Y 5BJ
HMS Belfast	SE1 2JH	Political Cartoon Gallery	WC1E 7QD	Vauxhall City Farm	SE11 5HS
Horse Guards Parade	SW1A 2AX	Pollocks Toy Museum	W1T 2HN	Victoria and Albert Museum	SW7 2RZ
Houses of Parliament	SW1A 2JX	Queen Elizabeth II Conference Centre	SW1P 3EE	Victoria Tower	SW1P 3JY
Hyde Park	W1K 7AN	Royal Academy of Arts	W1J 0BG	Waddington Galleries	W1S 3LT
Imperial War Museum	SE1 7PW	Royal Agricultural Hall	SW1P 2PA	Wallace Collection	W1U 3BN
Kensington Palace	W8 4PT	Royal Armouries	EC3N 4EE	Westminster Abbey	SW1P 3PP
London International Gallery of Children's Art	NW3 5HS	Royal College of Music Museum	SW7 5JE	Westminster Bridge	SW1A 2JH
Leicester Square	WC2H 7LH	Royal Exchange	EC3V 3ND	Westminster Cathedral	SW1P 1QE
Leighton House	W14 8NU			Winston Churchill Britain at War	SE1 2HP

Directory of Services

Advocacy, Advice & Information Groups

Blue Badge Network
01384 257001
headoffice@bluebadgenetwork.org.uk
www.bluebadgenetwork.org.uk
Championing the cause of disabled badge holders across the UK since 1991.

Dial UK
01302 310123
informationenquiries@dialuk.org.uk
www.dialuk.info
Provides information and advice to disabled people and others on all aspects of living with a disability.

Equality and Human Rights Commission
England   0845 604 6610
Scotland 0845 604 5510
Wales 0845 604 8810
englandhelpline@equalityhumanrights.com
www.equalityhumanrights.com
Champions equality and human rights for all, working to eliminate discrimination, reduce inequality, protect human rights and to build good relations, ensuring that everyone has a fair chance to participate in society.

National Centre for Independent Living
0845 026 4748
info@ncil.org.uk
www.ncil.org.uk
A national support, advice and consultancy organisation that aims to enable disabled people to be equal citizens with choice, control, rights and full economic, social and cultural lives.

Radar
020 7250 3222
radar@radar.org.uk
www.radar.org.uk
National network of disability organisations and disabled people. Members opinions and concerns are fast tracked to Westminster and Whitehall, and we launch our own campaigns to promote equality for all disabled people.

Ricability
020 7427 2460
mail@ricability.org.uk
www.ricability.org.uk
UK consumer research Charity providing free, practical unbiased reports for older and disabled people.

Scope
0808 800 33 33
response@scope.org.uk
www.scope.org.uk
An information, advice and support service to disabled people and their families. Contact us for information on cerebral palsy, disability issues and all of our services.

Transport for All
020 7737 2339
contactus@transportforall.org.uk
www.transportforall.org.uk
The voice of accessible transport users in London and campaigns for the right of disabled people to travel with the same freedom as non-disabled people. We represent users of door-to-door services like Dial-A-Ride and Taxicard.

Disability Organisations

AbilityNet
0800 269545
enquiries@abilitynet.org.uk
www.abilitynet.co.uk
A national charity helping disabled adults and children use computers and the internet by adapting and adjusting their technology.

Alzheimer's Society
0845 3000336 (Helpline)
enquiries@alzheimers.org.uk
www.alzheimers.org.uk
A membership organisation, which works to improve the quality of life of people affected by dementia in England, Wales and Northern Ireland.

Arthritis Care
0808 8004050 (Helpline)
Info@arthritiscare.org.uk
www.arthritiscare.org.uk
From high quality information and support to empower you to take control of your arthritis, to campaigning for change.

Ataxia
0845 6440606 (Helpline)
helpline@ataxia.org.uk
www.ataxla.org.uk
We provide help to all people affected by ataxia, a degenerative neurological condition. We offer free membership and support from first diagnosis to living with ataxia day to day.

BackCare
0845 130 2704 (Helpline)
info@backcare.org.uk
www.backcare.org.uk
BackCare is the charity that promotes healthier backs and helps people with back and neck pain. Our aim is to work alongside some of the most forward thinking individuals, organisations and companies to help us develop awareness of back and neck pain prevention.

British Polio Fellowship
0800 0180586 (Helpline)
info@britishpolio.org.uk
www.britishpolio.org.uk
The largest charity supporting people with polio or Post Polio Syndrome in the UK.

CMT United Kingdom
0800 6526316 (Helpline)
info@cmtuk.org.uk
www.cmt.org.uk
Working to support those who are affected by Charcot-Marie-Tooth disease, also known as Hereditary Motor and Sensory Neuropathy or Peroneal Muscular Atrophy.

Contact A Family
0808 808 3555 (Helpline)
info@cafamily.org.uk
www.cafamily.org.uk
The only UK-wide charity providing advice, information and support to the parents of all disabled children - no matter what their disability or health condition.

Deafblind UK
0800 132 320 (Helpline)
helpline@deafblind.org.uk
www.deafblind.org.uk
An organisation of and for people who are Deafblind or have a combined sight and hearing loss.

DebRA
01344 771961
debra@debra.org.uk
www.debra.org.uk
DebRA is the national charity working on behalf of people in the UK with the genetic skin blistering condition Epidermolysis Bullosa (EB).

Different Strokes
0845 130 7172
webcontact@differentstrokes.co.uk
www.differentstrokes.co.uk
A charity set up by younger stroke survivors for younger stroke survivors.

Disabled Living Foundation
0845 1309177 (Helpline)
helpline@dfl.org.uk
www.dlf.org.uk
The foundation provides free, impartial advice about all types of disability product and disabled equipment for older and disabled people, their carers and families.

Elizabeth Finn Care
0808 802 2000
info@elizabethfinn.org.uk
www.elizabethfinntrust.org.uk
Elizabeth Finn Care helps people who are struggling as a result of financial difficulties that have occurred through no fault of their own. It does this by providing direct financial support from Elizabeth Finn Grants together with information on how they can find additional help in the form of welfare benefits, charitable funds and other assistance available to them from the charity's Turn2us website and helpline services.

Haemophilia Society
0800 018 6068 (Helpline)
info@haemophilia.org.uk
www.haemophilia.org.uk
The society is working for people with
haemophilia, von Willebrand's or a related
bleeding disorder and their families to
secure the best possible care, treatment
and support.

Hemihelp
0845 123 2372 (Helpline)
info@hemihelp.org.uk
www.hemihelp.org.uk
A UK based charity for children and young
people with hemiplegia. Hemiplegia is a
neurological condition that weakens one
side of the body, and affects up to one
child in a thousand. Sometimes described
as a form of cerebral palsy with the effects
similar to a stroke.

Leonard Cheshire Disability
020 3242 0200
info@LCDisability.org
www.lcdisability.org
Principal activity in the UK is the provision
of services and support of disabled people
including care homes, supported living,
domiciliary support, day services, resource
centres, rehabilitation, respite care,
personal support, training and assistance
for those looking for work. The largest
voluntary sector provider of care and
support services for disabled people.

Limbless Association
0800 644 0185 (Helpline)
enquiries@limbless-association.org
www.limbless-association.org
The Limbless Association provides
information and support to the limb-loss
community. We aim to support people of
all ages and backgrounds through a variety
of existing programs and services; whether
they are about to have an amputation or
are already living with congenital or
acquired limb-loss. We also offer
assistance and information to carers, family
members and friends if they require it.

ME Association
0844 576 5326
meconnect@meassociation.org.uk
www.meassociation.org.uk
Providing information, support and
practical advice for people who are
affected by ME/CFS/PVFS (Myalgic
Encephalopathy/Chronic Fatigue
Syndrome/Post Viral Fatigue Syndrome),
their families and carers. We also fund and
support research, and offer education and
training.

Mencap
0808 808 1111 (Helpline)
help@mencap.org.uk
www.mencap.org.uk
Mencap is the UK's leading charity working
with people with a learning disability and
their families and carers. We campaign for
change at every level of government -
locally and nationally. We also provide a
wide range of services - housing,
education, employment and leisure - that
give people the chance to lead fulfilling,
active lives with as much independence as
possible.

Motor Neurone Disease Association
08457 626262 (Helpline)
enquiries@mndassociation.org
www.mndassociation.org
The Motor Neurone Disease Association
wants to see a world free of motor neurone
disease (MND). The leading charity
dedicated to MND funds cutting-edge
research within the UK and across the
world and works to ensure everyone with
MND receives the best care and support in
order to achieve the highest quality of life
possible.

Multiple Sclerosis Society
0808 800 8000 (Helpline)
helpline@mssociety.org.uk
www.mssociety.org.uk
The UK's largest charity for people affected
by Multiple Sclerosis (MS) - about 85,000
people in the UK.

Parkinson's UK
0808 800 0303 (Helpline)
hello@parkinsons.org.uk
www.parkinsons.org.uk
We're the Parkinson's support and research charity. Help us find a cure and improve life for everyone affected by Parkinson's.

Restricted Growth Association
0300 111 1970
office@restrictedgrowth.co.uk
www.restrictedgrowth.co.uk
UK based charity that provides vital information and support to improve the quality of life for persons of restricted growth, and their families.

Shape Arts
020 7424 7330
info@shapearts.org.uk
www.shapearts.org.uk
Shape is the country's leading disability arts organisation, we aim to improve access to the arts for deaf and disabled people whilst supporting deaf and disabled artists to challenge perceptions and promote Deaf and Disability Culture.

Spinal Injuries Association
0800 980 0501
sia@spinal.co.uk
www.spinal.co.uk
SIA was set up in 1974 in order to support people with SCI. The founders themselves had SCI and, to this day, SIA is run by a board of trustees who live with spinal cord injury.

Stroke Association
0303 3033 100
info@stroke.org.uk
www.stroke.org.uk
The only UK wide charity solely concerned with combating strokes in people of all ages. It funds research into prevention, treatment and better methods of rehabilitation, and helps stroke patients and their families directly through its helpline and Life after Stroke Services.

The Thalidomide Trust
01480 474074
administration@thalidomidetrust.org
www.thalidomidc.org.uk
The aim of the Trust is to provide relief and assistance for those people born in the UK, damaged as a result of their mothers having taken the drug Thalidomide (as manufactured by Distillers Biochemicals Limited) during their pregnancy.

Motoring Related Information & Organisations

BBC London Travel News London
0330 123 0184
travel.news@bbc.co.uk
bbc.co.uk/travelnews/london
Updates every 15/30 minutes if you spot travel incidents.

Disabled Motoring UK
01508 489 449
enquiries@disabledmotoring.org
www.disabledmotoring.org
UK charity that promotes mobility for disabled people. We represent the interests of disabled drivers, passengers, scooter & wheelchair users, as well as their friends, families and carers.

Disabled Motorists Federation
0191 4163172
peter@dmfed.org.uk
www.dmfed.ork.uk
The Disabled Motorists Federation (registered charity No 1012874) aims to create more inclusive and equal societies for disabled people as well as their carers and families.The federation also wants to increase the number of existing relationships it already has with certain central and local government departments and commercial companies.

Driver & Vehicle Licensing Agency (DVLA)
0845 712 3456
drivers@.dvla@gtnet.gov.uk
www.direct.gov.uk/en/disabledpeople
Road tax exemption for disabled people.

Highways Agency
0300 123 5000
ha_info@highways.gsi.gov.uk
www.highways.gov.uk
An Executive Agency of the Department for Transport (DfT) responsible for operating, maintaining and improving the strategic road network in England on behalf of the Secretary of State for Transport.

Motability
0845 456 4566
correspondence@motabilityoperations.co.uk
www.motability.co.uk
Wide range of cars available cheaply and easily through lease or hire purchase.

Parking and Traffic Appeals Service (PATAS)
020 7520 7200
www.parkingandtrafficappeals.gov.uk
For parking, bus lane, moving traffic charge notices, or congestion charge zone penalty charge notices, and information about the Parking and Traffic Appeals Service.

Queen Elizabeth's Foundation Mobility Centre
020 8770 1151
mobility@qef.org.uk
www.qef.org.uk
Helpline and tuition for disabled people who wish to learn to drive.

Trace
0845 206 8602
Towed Away? Clamped? 24 hour helpline.

Tourism & Access

Calvert Trust
Lake District 01768 772255
Kielder 01434 250232
Exmoor 01598 763221
www.calvert-trust.org.uk
The trust has been enabling people with disabilities, together with their families and friends, to achieve their potential through outdoor adventure activities in the countryside.

Fieldfare Trust
01334 657708
info@fieldfare.org.uk
www.fieldfare.org.uk
Works with people with disabilities and countryside managers to improve access to the countryside for everyone.

National Trust Access for All
01793 817634
enquiries@nationaltrust.org.uk
www.nationaltrust.org.uk
On-going commitment to accessibility in all areas of its work. We strive to achieve this in many ways: improving access to and around our properties; making it easy for people of all abilities to join our staff or volunteer teams; allowing everyone access to our information and interpretation.

Tourism for All UK
0303 303 0146
info@tourismforall.org.uk
www.tourismforall.org.uk
Tourism for All UK is an independent charity supporting leisure and tourism opportunities for all, operating an information service to older and disabled people, and working with the industry and government to raise the standards of welcome to all guests. OpenBritain is their consumer brand.

Directory of Services

Wheelyboat Trust
01798 342222
info@wheelyboats.org
www.wheelyboats.org
A registered charity dedicated to providing disabled people with the freedom to participate in waterborne activities all over the UK. Our principal role is to help public venues, groups and organisations acquire wheelchair accessible Wheelyboats for the benefit of their disabled visitors, members, beneficiaries, etc.

Travel by Bus/Taxi/Tube

Capital Call
020 7275 2446
capitalcall@hackneyct.org
www.tfl.gov.uk
Subsidised door-to-door transport for people with mobility issues using private hire vehicles (minicabs). Please note that this service is only available to London residents within certain boroughs.

Department for Transport
0300 330 3000
FAX9643@dft.gsi.gov.uk
www.dft.gov.uk
Aims to deliver a transport system that balances the needs of the economy, the environment and society. Contact us for further information on Blue Badge Scheme Policy and using the Blue Badge in Europe.

Dial-a-Ride
020 7309 8900
Dar.generalenquiries@tfl.gov.uk
www.tfl.gov.uk
A free door-to-door service for disabled people who can't use buses, trains or the tube.

Freedom Pass
0845 275 7054
www.londoncouncils.gov.uk/services/freedompass
The concessionary travel scheme in London for eligible older and disabled

residents, whose sole or principal residence is in a London borough. It allows free travel on buses, Tube, trains, London Overground, Docklands Light Railway and trams in London and on local buses in England.

London Taxi & Private Hire
0845 300 7000
www.tfl.gov.uk/findaride
Responsible for the licensing of taxi and private hire, including minicab services in London.

London Travel Information
0843 222 1234
www.tfl.gov.uk
One-stop shop for information on tickets and travelling around London.

Taxicard Scheme
0845 415 4156
Taxicard@londoncouncils.gov.uk
www.londoncouncils.gov.uk/services/taxicard
Subsidised door to door transport in licensed taxis and private hire vehicles for residents of London boroughs who have mobility impairments, and who find it difficult to use mainstream public transport.

Have your say

Since we published the first edition of this guide we have welcomed your comments about the content and taken on board your suggestions. As a result we have increased the area of mapping to reflect the next generation of living and working in the Capital.

Feedback

We appreciate your valuable feedback and support with this Guide. If there are any specific items you would like to see in future editions please email us with your comments at **support@thePIEguide.com**

Parking in London

If you have any general comments about parking in London, you can contact London Councils by emailing **parking@londoncouncils.gov.uk**, by phoning **020 7934 9999** or by writing to **Transport and Mobility Services, London Councils, 59 ½ Southwark Street, London SE1 0AL**.

Changes

We have worked very hard to compile and update the comprehensive information in this Guide and realise how quickly things can change. If you notice any changes on your travels we would be pleased to hear from you by email at **support@thePIEguide.com**

Purchase Maps

To purchase this and other PIE guides, maps or useful items visit our website at **www.thePIEguide.com/shop**, phone **0844 847 0875** or email **orders@thePIEguide.com**

www.parkingforbluebadges.com

Resellers and Distributors

For enquiries to resell this and other guides contact PIE directly on **0844 847 0875** or email **orders@thePIEguide.com**

About us

PIE produces customised data for publishing, websites and satnav devices for different community groups e.g. Blue Badge holders, van drivers and motorcyclists. We can license the data or create a bespoke product for you, whatever your needs. For further information contact **0844 847 0875**.